Vested
OUTSOURCING

Vested OUTSOURCING

Five Rules That Will *Transform* Outsourcing

Kate Vitasek
with
Mike Ledyard and Karl Manrodt

VESTED OUTSOURCING
Copyright © Kate Vitasek, 2010.

First published in 2010 by
PALGRAVE MACMILLAN®
in the United States—a division of St. Martin's Press LLC,
175 Fifth Avenue, New York, NY 10010.

Where this book is distributed in the UK, Europe and the rest of the
world, this is by Palgrave Macmillan, a division of Macmillan Publishers
Limited, registered in England, company number 785998, of Houndmills,
Basingstoke, Hampshire RG21 6XS.

Palgrave Macmillan is the global academic imprint of the above companies
and has companies and representatives throughout the world.

Palgrave® and Macmillan® are registered trademarks in the United States,
the United Kingdom, Europe and other countries.

ISBN: 978–0–230–62317–0

Library of Congress Cataloging-in-Publication Data

Vitasek, Kate.
    Vested outsourcing / Kate Vitasek, Mike Ledyard.
        p. cm.
    Includes index.
    ISBN 978–0–230–62317–0
        1. Contracting out. I. Ledyard, Mike. II. Title.

HD2365.V58 2010
658.4′058—dc22   2009032314

A catalogue record of the book is available from the British Library.

Design by Newgen Imaging Systems (P) Ltd., Chennai, India.

First edition: February 2010

10 9 8 7 6 5 4 3 2 1

Printed in the United States of America.

DEDICATION

We would like to dedicate this book to our spouses, who have selflessly given us time, support, and encouragement throughout our careers. We are believers that win-win principles are a foundation for success in our personal lives. Our marriages are a testament that together is indeed better.

Greg, Kris, and Susan: We are in your debt, and appreciate all that you have done for us. We look forward with love to being together for many years to come.

Greg Picinich
Vested to Kate Vitasek since May 17, 2003

Kris Ledyard
Vested to Mike Ledyard since June 9, 1973

Susan Manrodt
Vested to Karl Manrodt since June 12, 1982

CONTENTS

FIGURES

INTRODUCTION

The significant problems we face cannot be solved at the same level of thinking we were at when we created them.
—Albert Einstein

IS THERE A BETTER WAY?

No other question encapsulates the drive for continuous improvement permeating today's business environment. It is what drives people like Albert Einstein and Thomas Edison to challenge the status quo to create not just better products but also better solutions. It is what drives businesspeople to solve complex problems to meet customer needs.

Finding a better way is what challenges the music industry to reinvent how the industry delivers music to users, shifting from albums, to eight-track tapes, to cassettes, to CDs, and now to MP3 files. But finding a better way is not just a question that inventors, technologists, and engineers are asking.

Today's outsourcing professionals are starting to ask themselves the same question. Progressive companies are starting to challenge conventional outsourcing approaches and tools in search of a better way. In fact, the challenges are so significant that Frank Casale, chief executive officer of the Outsourcing Institute, describes the twenty-first century as the tipping point for companies to begin to explore alternative approaches and tools for outsourcing—what he calls Outsourcing 2.0.

What exactly is the better way to outsource? That is the question that the University of Tennessee asked when it created a small research team—the authors of this book—to study outsourcing practices. In fact, the question was so intriguing that the United States Air Force, which spends more than 50 percent of its entire procurement budget on procured services, agreed to sponsor the research study.

Through the University of Tennessee research efforts, we have studied progressive companies that were exploring more innovative approaches to outsourcing. We found several common themes in the companies we researched, regardless of the types of services outsourced. One of the key themes found across all of the companies was the shift away from a conventional customer-supplier relationship to a highly collaborative relationship aimed at developing a broad, true win-win solution.

We have taken our collective wisdom as practitioners and academics, coupled with our research, and distilled the lessons learned into a systematic model to improve outsourcing as a business practice. We call this model Vested Outsourcing™ because the core principle is creating outsourcing relationships where companies and their suppliers become vested in each other's success. Vested Outsourcing is a fresh approach to outsourcing that will drive benefits for both the company outsourcing and its outsource providers.

Vested Outsourcing is a defining element of Outsourcing 2.0. In conventional outsourcing, the customer attempts to reduce costs while the service provider attempts to increase the size of the contract. Following the Vested Outsourcing rules results in creating innovative solutions that resolves these conflicting goals. In a Vested Outsourcing deal, the economics of the business model are structured so that the company that is outsourcing reduces its costs while maintaining or increasing service levels and the service provider improves its profits. Implementing Vested Outsourcing will improve the outsourcing process much the way Six Sigma and Lean improved production processes in the 1980s and 1990s.

Our goal in writing this book is to encourage outsourcing professionals—including those in companies that outsource and those at service providers—that they should take Albert Einstein's advice if they are to find a better way to outsource. We hope that after reading this book, you question your organization's conventional transactional-based outsourcing business models. We hope that you will understand there is a better way to outsource.

You might ask yourself if this book is for you. If you play a role in the outsourcing profession and are looking for a better way to outsource, then it is. This book is targeted for both the companies that outsource and the outsource providers, educators, and consultants who are working to teach companies a better way to outsource.

Last, we want to make it clear that this book is not an attempt to convince you of the merits of outsourcing or to help you determine the kinds of activities to outsource. We assume you are already outsourcing or know that you want to outsource. For those wanting to learn the basics about when and what to outsource, we recommend a book called *SmartSourcing* by Thomas Koulopoulos and Tom Roloff,[1] or other resources, such as the Outsourcing Institute (www.outsourcing.com) or the International Association of Outsourcing Professionals (www. outsourcingprofessional.org).

OVERVIEW OF THE STRUCTURE OF THIS BOOK

We want to share the key findings of our experiences as practitioners and educators about how to improve outsourcing. We have distilled these experiences and research into the Vested Outsourcing business model companies can follow to take their outsourcing relationships to a higher level. This book is divided into three sections.

Part I sets the stage of the dynamics behind conventional outsourcing. It is designed to provide the reader with a better understanding of why companies need to develop an outsourcing business model whereby the company outsourcing and its service providers go the whole nine yards to deliver the best solution to solve today's business problems. We then step back and take a look at the evolution of outsourcing and challenge companies to rethink how their own outsourcing business models have evolved. We end Part I by building awareness of the ten most common ailments we see in conventional outsourcing relationships.

In Part II, we explore how Vested Outsourcing works. We prescribe in depth five rules of developing a Vested Outsourcing relationship. By applying these rules, you can take your outsourcing relationships to a higher level with improved results. We then explore two fundamental economic principles that are the driving forces behind a Vested Outsourcing solution: behavioral economics and the economics of innovation. Using these two principles, companies can structure Vested Outsourcing arrangements that encourage outsource providers to develop innovative solutions to solve business problems, not just perform tasks.

In Part III, we lay out the comprehensive steps to get started, all the way to transitioning the existing business to the new Vested Outsourcing business model. Each chapter is devoted to one of the implementation steps needed as you take your journey to a better way of outsourcing.

A NOTE ON TERMINOLOGY

Before we go the whole nine yards, it is important to understand what outsourcing is and what can be outsourced. *Outsourcing* refers to the transfer of a process or function to an external provider. When referring to the Air Force research, we sometimes use the term *services acquisition* instead of outsourcing.

In today's market, almost anything can be outsourced. Types of services being outsourced range from technical support, call centers, third-party logistics and distribution services, aircraft maintenance, product returns and food service, to facilities management for an entire campus of buildings. Usually, if a process is not core to the organization, it is a candidate for outsourcing.

We also want to point out that we use the terms *procure, source, purchase, buy,* and *acquisition* interchangeably. In all cases, the terms are meant in the context of a company that is buying outsourced services.

We also refer to the parties involved in an outsource agreement. We refer to the company that is outsourcing as the *outsourcing company,* the *customer,* or the *client.* The provider of these services is referred to as the *outsource service provider, outsource provider,* or *supplier.* The terms are used interchangeably to reduce redundancy.

Finally, we use the terms *relationship, partnership,* and *arrangement* interchangeably to refer to the coming together of a company that is outsourcing with one or more of its service providers under a common contract. All of the examples we explore in this book are between two parties, but we have seen Vested Outsourcing relationships that involve more than one service provider.

With that as background, it is time to start the journey of understanding Vesting Outsourcing.

PART I

DIAGNOSING THE NEED

CHAPTER 1

THE WHOLE NINE YARDS

THE LESSON OF GIVING THINGS YOUR ALL

In 1994, I* was given the challenge to develop a worldwide outsourcing strategy for Microsoft's marketing programs. At the time, Microsoft was a $4 billion company working to realize Bill Gates's vision of putting a computer on every person's desk. In order for Microsoft to achieve this objective, it needed to reach as many people as possible through as many venues as possible, so marketing was a big deal at Microsoft. The company was hiring the best and brightest marketing talent in the business and was challenging them to come up with new ways to reach customers all over the world, resulting in creative new "Marketing Programs" as a key way to reach potential customers. More than a dozen marketing programs had emerged, each needing a different set of operational requirements. Some of these included:

- Disk and document fulfillment
- Courseware program
- Microsoft Certified Professionals
- "Select" corporate licensing program

These were just a sampling of some of Microsoft's new programs at this time. The programs were great for sales, but operationally speaking, they were a nightmare because each marketing program had different customers, in different parts of the world, with different operational requirements and materials to send to program customers. To help solve these problems, Microsoft turned to dozens of outsource providers worldwide.

Like many companies, Microsoft found itself using various service providers to perform a wide range of services. Yet Microsoft did not have a formal outsourcing process. To solve this problem, it brought in a team of experts and consultants to review the process: I was one of those experts. Microsoft later hired me to help implement the outsourcing operations for three of its largest marketing programs. My primary goal was to get the absolute best service levels from our service providers at the absolute best price. Of course, I gave it my all to achieve this goal.

Fast forward to 1997. I decided to leave Microsoft and join Stream International—at the time one of Microsoft's largest outsource partners. Stream International was a $1 billion-plus outsource service provider in customer care, technical support, and manufacturing and distribution in the high-tech sector.[1] It managed some of Microsoft's most complex outsourcing problems, including much of its corporate licensing fulfillment worldwide.

At Stream International, I led a team that would implement the large sales deals sold by the company's sales reps. It was a common joke among the operational folks at Stream International that the opportunistic sales reps would sell "vaporware." In the outsourcing profession, *vaporware* is a term used to describe services that were not fully in place at the service provider. It was my team's job to figure out how to deliver what the sales reps had sold without customers realizing they had bought vaporware.

The sales reps and the legal team would negotiate the deal, and the goal was always the same: Sell as much as you can with the highest profit margin possible. This would maximize revenue and preserve profit margins. In almost all cases, Stream International charged its clients a price for each "activity" performed, which was customary for the industry. For example, there was a cost per minute to answer calls and provide technical support to the clients' customers. There was a cost per "touch" to manufacture the customer's product. There was a price per pallet to store the customer's product. In short, the more activities we performed, the more money Stream International got paid. And since the sales reps were on a commission plan, the more revenue they booked, the more they got paid. If the customer pressed for lower prices in one area, it was the sales rep's job to shift the pricing around to keep Stream International's profit margin "whole." As such, the sales reps gave it their all to maximize revenue and profitability for the firm because when the company won, they personally won.

Once the work was implemented, it was managed by what Stream International called a business manager, who had profit and loss (P&L) responsibility for that account. The goal was simple: Meet customer service levels and meet P&L targets. Business managers had to live with the clients for daily interactions, so for the most part, they would give their customers their all to make the customers happy; as a result, the company was a customer service oriented firm.

Customers would repeatedly ask business managers to bring proactive ideas to make the business better. After all, the customers had outsourced to the experts! One of two interesting dynamics would occur.

The first dynamic had to do with the type of ideas that were generated. First, if the business manager found ways to bring efficiency to the client, management often frowned because it would reduce revenue. When a smaller number of activities are performed, revenue is lower, or when the cost to perform services decreases, revenue decreases. Being efficient was just bad business. Over time, a culture developed where business managers would focus their improvement ideas on areas that would generate more revenue for Stream International. These revenue-generating ideas were termed *value-added activities*. For example, the business manager would work to deliver same-day service (for orders received by the client, to meet last minute changes to an order, etc.). Or he or she would offer to develop a solution for physical destruction and disposal of the client's inventory when the client eliminated certain stock-keeping units. Although these ideas solved a customer's problem, they almost always came with a charge associated with the activity. A good business manager at Stream International was very clever at identifying ways to perform an activity that would solve a client's problem. Once again, business managers gave it their all. Stream International solved the problem, and in return, it was rewarded with billable activity. More activity meant more revenue.

The second dynamic between Stream International and its clients also evolved over time. When a business manager developed an idea that would have a positive impact for clients, clients often discounted the idea or chose *not* to approve the improvement initiative. The reason was twofold.

First, clients often said, "That is not the way we did the work before. We would like you to keep doing it the same way as we have outlined in our standard operating procedures." In essence, the clients had outsourced to the experts, but they were not open-minded to change the way the work was done.

The second reason clients gave for not wanting to approve improvement initiatives was because they would have to get another group involved that controlled that part of the process. For example, one business manager pointed out that the client's bill of materials, which outlined the manufacturing guidelines, often was wrong—as much as 80 percent of the time. The situation was so problematic that it became customary for the business management team to create a new bill of materials based on its expertise in order to produce the client's product correctly. This work was not in scope. The client's vendor account manager had tried, to no avail, to get the client's marketing people to improve their internal process and correct the issues with their bills of materials. The vendor account manager finally solved the problem by allowing Stream International to charge a value-added service to redo the bill of materials rather than work with the marketing people within the client to create a proper bill of materials. This meant that bills of materials were produced twice, once incorrectly by the client and then again by Stream International.

THE WHACK-A-MOLE APPROACH TO OUTSOURCING

If everyone was giving it their all, what was the problem?

Over and over through many new projects, I witnessed the same dynamics. The client would want the best service at the lowest cost per activity. The service provider would want the highest margin and lots of activities in order to maximize revenue and profits. If Stream International was pushed to reduce its margin, smart people would work to sell more activities. Once the work was implemented, the focus was on maintaining the P&L for the service provider. It was capitalism and free market economy at its best. Clients would win if they were able to reduce their costs. Stream International would win if it was able to maximize its revenue and profits. The problem, as I saw it, was that while each party was giving it their all individually, the overall solution was far from optimized.

Through my observations, I recognized that solutions to particular problems often seem to create activities and expenses rather than eliminate them. For example, on the surface in the case just mentioned, the problem of having bad bills of materials was solved. But in reality, the problem was merely masked. A permanent fix to the accuracy of how bills of material were being created was what really was needed. Instead of fixing the real problem, Stream International was paid to fix the symptoms. The reason for these seemingly paradoxical solutions was that often it is much easier to fix symptoms than causes. People on both sides of the outsourcing equation were putting a Band-Aid on the symptoms rather than fixing the root cause of problems. Decisions were made in a vacuum to optimize the individual firm's goals rather than looking at the total picture.

I came to call my observation the mole theory because the effects were similar to the Whack-a-Mole game children play. When a child whacks the mole in the game, the mole is never really eliminated but is chased somewhere else. My view was that companies were reacting to their problems like a child reacts in the Whack-a-Mole game: giving it their all each time a mole popped up before them but never permanently eliminating the mole. Unfortunately, in most cases, the people could not see the entire process. The result was that the problem—the mole—simply popped up somewhere else, which was almost always out of their line of sight and span of control.

The problem was simple. Everyone was working to achieve what was in their own best interest rather to work together for a much broader definition of success.

THE COMPLETE COLLABORATIVE RELATIONSHIP

By nature, the company that is outsourcing and the service provider have the same goal: to make profit. However, they approach this goal from opposite viewpoints. Cost to the company that is outsourcing is revenue to the service provider.

My premise: *Create a business model where both the company that outsources and the service provider are able to maximize their profits.* Doing this means creating a culture where both parties work together to make the end-to-end process efficient regardless of what party is performing activities. *This means creating an approach where service providers are rewarded for* reducing *their revenue.*

To be successful, companies would have to change the lens through which they look at problems. I turned to my supply chain background and saw a model for a new approach in classic Lean principles. Pioneered by Toyota, Lean is a process improvement method that stresses eliminating all activities that do not add value to a process. Unfortunately, most organizations have applied this thinking rather narrowly, such as at a manufacturing plant or warehouse.

My plan was to convey Lean concepts across the *entire* supply chain and to make improvements in the end-to-end solution regardless of who was performing an activity. In short, my plan would pay the outsource provider to meet service levels while making the overall operations of what is being outsourced as efficient as possible. The more efficient the process, the more profit the outsource provider (or providers, if more than one were involved) would make.

Under my vision, companies and people would not be rewarded for giving their all to solve their immediate problem and improve their individual position. I would come to call my thinking the Three Musketeers' approach which fostered an environment of "all for one, one for all." When everyone worked together toward an optimized solution, everyone would benefit. All for one, one for all. I had the opportunity to test some of my theories, on companies large and small, when I founded Supply Chain Visions, Ltd., a consulting firm, in 2002. Supply Chain Visions is recognized by ARC Advisory Group as one of the Top 10 boutique consulting firms specializing in supply chain management.

Fast forward to 2003. Dr. Alex Miller, the dean for the Center of Executive Education at the University of Tennessee (UT), was spearheading a five-year, $25 million research contract for the United States Air Force to study many aspects of its supply chain. UT has long been known as a leader in supply chain management and logistics.[2] A key area that the Air Force wanted UT to explore was how to improve procurement for the logistics and maintenance support for its weapon systems. To put the problem in perspective, it was not uncommon for Air Force contracts for logistics and maintenance to exceed $1 billion.

Dr. Miller was particularly intrigued with my experience in outsourcing and performance management and asked me to lead the research effort. Our research began by examining how the Air Force procured its logistics and maintenance support; later the project grew in scope and focus to help the Air Force understand how it could procure *any* of the services it outsourced. Outsourcing (known as service acquisition in the Air Force) is big business because it spends more than 50 percent of its budget on services, totaling over $63 billion annually.[3]

Our research involved looking at both the process of procuring outsourced services and examining actual contracts. It also involved field interviews with Air Force procurement and program teams as well as with service providers.

What we found was that the business model and the relationship in outsourcing deals often have fundamental flaws. The flaws result in direct negative or unconscious behaviors that drive unintended consequences.

A key component of our research was to go beyond simply studying the Air Force's issues and to find a better way for it to outsource. Through our efforts, we had the opportunity to study progressive companies that were exploring innovative approaches to outsourcing, working with companies that were outsourcing as well as outsource providers. We studied successful outsourcing arrangements that existed within the Department of Defense as well as in the commercial sector. For example, we had the opportunity to study the General Electric (GE) F404 Engine program, a $10 billion engine maintenance and repair contract for the Navy in which the joint GE and Navy team had been recognized for excellence by the Office of the Secretary of Defense.[4]

On the commercial side, we had the opportunity to learn from Jaguar and Unipart, which had been recognized by ARC Advisory Group for their innovative approaches to solving Jaguar's spare parts distribution problem.[5] Throughout the various phases of our research project, we examined more than 50 outsourced solutions spanning logistics, maintenance, facilities management, cafeteria management, and information technology services.

Our work resulted in the development of detailed courseware that was aimed at fundamentally changing the process and culture of how the Air Force procured services. We were able to test our implementation approaches and concepts with different Air Force programs, refining our thinking along the way. Our work ultimately became the foundation for courseware that is now being taught by the Defense Acquisition University (DAU) and is being rolled out by the Air Force. The DAU is the corporate university for the DoD's acquisition workforce.

THE TIPPING POINT FOR OUTSOURCING

The pioneering industrialist Henry Ford once observed, "Coming together is the beginning. Keeping together is progress. Working together is success." But in the world of outsourcing, working together for success can be a significant challenge. This is especially true where businesses working together face the same goal: maximizing their own revenues and profits. But just because this is a challenge, it should not mean that companies should throw in the hat and bring the work back in house. Some companies are indeed deciding that outsourcing is not worth its benefits and are taking the work back inside. In 2006, Sprint Nextel sued IBM for $6 million, claiming that IBM had not lived up to expectations on an information technology contract. Sprint Nextel rehired some workers and reduced the work submitted under the contract; yet, despite the challenges, Sprint Nextel did not throw in the hat, and continued to outsource with IBM.[6] The men's apparel brand Joseph Aboud recently studied the impact of bringing back in-house some of the work previously done by its third-party logistics provider.[7] But, as we explore in chapter 2, outsourcing is here to stay. The challenge then becomes how to outsource better.

Frank Casale, chief executive of the Outsourcing Institute, agrees. He describes the dynamics of today's outsourcing environment as being at a tipping point. "Outsourcing has had a permanent effect on today's business. However, we are rapidly approaching a tipping point in the outsourcing marketplace, the impact of which will be significant and far reaching. I refer to this imminent inflection point as *Outsourcing 2.0*. Like any movement, as it gathers momentum, it becomes hard to ignore."[8]

In the twenty-first century, it is imperative to challenge the conventional approaches to outsourcing and develop truly collaborative relationships where all parties are vested in the overall success of the entire solution, not just their own part.

The good news is that it seems Henry Ford's wisdom is starting to get traction. Today the business world is abuzz about "collaboration." However, as I learned from my days at Microsoft and Stream International and validated with our Air Force research, true collaboration and outsourcing are often at odds with each other. Businesses and organizations cooperate with one another but typically do so halfheartedly and guardedly. To each party in the agreement, its individual success is paramount, and often in direct conflict because the cost to the company that is outsourcing is revenue to the service provider. When one achieves their profit goals, it is often at the expense of the other.

It is crucial to develop an outsourced collaboration model where the economics work for all parties involved. Those economics need to drive behavioral changes that are powerful enough to promote win-win versus win-lose solutions. In Vested Outsourcing, the golden rule is that a company outsourcing should not win at the expense of its service provider, and vice versa. The economics of the collaborative business model should be so powerful that it drives efforts to solve for an optimized, complete solution.

GOING THE WHOLE NINE YARDS

Vested Outsourcing combines the four influential business concepts of the twenty-first century: outsourcing, collaboration, innovation, and measurement. Like Lean, it is about streamlining and eliminating non-value-added activities regardless of who is doing work. But Vested Outsourcing goes well beyond applying Lean principles; it pushes the companies involved in an outsource relationship to innovate collaboratively to find the optimized solution, even if it means trade-offs for one of the parties involved. At its heart, Vested Outsourcing is about all parties in the business arrangement going the whole nine yards to unlock the most efficient and effective solutions to work being performed.

But what does it truly mean to go "the whole nine yards"? Although linguists debate the etymological origins of the phrase, they agree that it refers to entirety, to the full extent of something. The phrase metaphorically symbolizes that anything less than nine yards is an *incomplete* effort.[9] Likewise, unless all the parties in an outsourced arrangement work together under identical principles and with identical objectives, success will be elusive.

The world has changed. As Frank Casale points out, the world of outsourcing as we know it is about to change too. At a time when the public image of America's corporate leadership is tainted amid accusations of self-centered excesses, there is a renaissance of what we have all intuitively known: the return of business models based on collaboration, innovation, and everyone winning. Vested Outsourcing is a fresh approach to solve for today's outsourcing problems. Going the whole nine yards reflects a relationship that is collaborative, symbiotic, and mutually beneficial.

As businesses find themselves at the inflection point between conventional outsourcing models and Outsourcing 2.0, we believe more and more companies will start to reflect on what it truly means to go the whole nine yards with their outsource relationships. A secondary meaning of going the whole nine yards is: *For you I'll go the whole nine yards. You are worth the whole nine yards.* That is perfect reflection of a shift from "us versus them" to a "we" philosophy, which results in the ultimate successful business relationship.

CHAPTER 2

AN OUTSOURCING PRIMER

B usiness outsourcing as a concept has been around for decades. Many credit the technology services provider EDS as the pioneer for popularizing the use of the term *outsourcing* several decades ago to describe its service to run and maintain large mainframe computers and data centers. Others say the term has its roots in the movement in the 1970s to have outside companies manufacture some or all of product production. Still others say outsourcing is just a variation of sourcing goods and services. No matter what the derivation of the word, outsourcing is firmly part of today's modern vocabulary.

Outsourcing has its roots in our collective past of human development in commerce and trade. Its history runs parallel with the history of civilization and open trade. As individuals formed family clans, then small groups, communities, and complex societies, individual members of society began to specialize. That led to a division of labor, improved skill and knowledge, and better workmanship. People with specialized skills would trade with each other for goods and services they needed to survive. They did not try to be totally self-sufficient; they used the talents and productivity of others and as a result lived better.

Much of humanity's progress is due to this division of labor. The seminal capitalist and economist Adam Smith wrote in the *Wealth of Nations* in 1776 that "the greatest improvement in the productive powers of labor, and the greater part of the skill, dexterity, and judgment with which it is anywhere directed, or applied, seem to have been the effects of the division of labor."[1] The division of labor is the foundation of Smith's theories of growth and prosperity and of his theories of international trade. The general concept that Smith advanced was that when workers focused on a limited number of tasks or processes, they improved their skill and their productivity. When skilled workers divided the task of production, output was far greater than when one individual tried to perform all tasks. This observation is just as true today on the factory floor or in the back office.

At its core, outsourcing can be viewed as a form of this division of labor. When tasks are given to companies that have the best skills to perform them, productivity is higher and economic resources are better utilized. The decision to outsource is fundamentally one of company structure or the setting of boundaries of what production or service the company will produce and make available to its customers. In the 1900s, most companies focused on horizontal or vertical integration. They wanted to build economies of scale, exercise greater market power, expand their product ranges, or gain control over resources.[2] But this strategy drove underperformance and made companies slow to react to changes in the market and technology.

The early outsourcing agreements of the 1970s, when manufacturers began contracting out the production of components to smaller, specialized suppliers, can be considered extensions in raw material or component sourcing. These agreements tended to be simple and focused on specifications, quality, and price. In the 1980s, many companies began to outsource a few business processes, such as accounting services, payroll, billing, and word processing. Companies would detail the job function to a third party, and the interactions were fairly simple. Outsourcing agreements were somewhat limited in scope and often focused primarily on lowering costs.

In the 1990s, a new way of thinking emerged regarding company structure. Companies began to focus on their core business and on reducing transaction costs. Peters and Waterman popularized the concept of a core competency in the book *In Search of Excellence*.[3] Hamel and Prahalad further popularized the concept in the widely read article "The Core Competence of the Corporation."[4] Business journals and boardrooms were abuzz with talk of focusing on the "company's core"; business strategies shifted; and talk of shedding noncore processes and even entire business units was the order of the day. This strategy of focusing on core competency is credited with unleashing the wave of outsourcing growth in the 1990s.

Outsourcing would not have made much headway as a strategy if not for improvements in information technology (IT) and
the way IT enabled companies to communicate quickly and easily
over vast distances. Thomas Friedman, in his book *The World Is Flat*,
observed that outsourcing is made possible by the massive investment in technology, with hundreds of millions of dollars invested in
broadband connectivity around the world.[5] It is this investment that
allowed work to be split up into chunks and tasks to be shared without regard to borders or distances. In essence, technology changed
the face of the workplace; work did not have to be in the same office
building, region, or time zone, making work "placeless." Broadband
connectivity drove the swell of outsourcing in "knowledge-based"
processes such as IT, design engineering, and call center operations,
and many other processes once thought too difficult to outsource
became candidates. These events accelerated the change in the business landscape and were taking place just as the new millennium
began. Michael Corbett speaks of this in *The Outsourcing Revolution*:
"In many ways, outsourcing may well prove to be the key enabler of
the 21st-century global economy."[6] We agree; outsourcing *is* revolu-
tionary, and it will continue to evolve and change how we define businesses in this century.

The term *outsourcing* is used broadly and encompasses many types
of services. There is scarcely any activity that cannot be outsourced.
Business segments typically outsourced include IT, human resources,
facilities, real estate management, logistics/warehousing services, and
accounting. Many companies also outsource customer support and
call center functions, including telemarketing, computer-aided drafting, customer service, market research, manufacturing, designing,
web development, content writing, ghostwriting, and engineering.
Companies are seeking to outsource any process that is not deemed
as core to their business. As Tom Peters says, "Do what you do best and
outsource the rest."[7]

As the range of what is being outsourced expands, so too is the
scope of the work being outsourced. Today's outsourcing solutions
range from offshore labor, to partial outsourcing (e.g., outsourcing an
asset), to business process outsourcing (BPO), all the way to what some
call full outsourcing, which includes the complete outsourcing of assets,
people, business processes, and management of an area of the enterprise, all under the same contract.[8]

As the scope of activities has expanded—especially to include off-shore labor—many have come to identify outsourcing with jobs shipped overseas and rising unemployment. Even though the terms *outsourcing* and *offshoring* are at times used interchangeably, there are very important and real differences. Outsourcing involves contracting with an outside supplier, which may or may not involve moving the work offshore. Jobs might be lost in a specific company, but the jobs might not move offshore and be lost to the home country's economy. Offshoring, however, is the transfer of work to another country, regardless of whether the work is outsourced to an outside supplier or stays within the same company.

But just how big is the outsourcing market? Estimating the actual size of the total outsourcing market is difficult. The Bureau of Economic Analysis (BEA), the analysis arm of the United States Department of Commerce, said in a March 2008 report on outsourcing that "no apparent consensus exists in the economics profession on how to define outsourcing and international standards provide little guidance on how to treat outsourcing in national economic accounts." The BEA has a number of research papers dedicated to outsourcing in the works, with reports due to Congress in early 2010. At that time, there could be more fact-based estimates of the total outsourcing industry. Until then, one of the better estimates we have found is the most recent estimate by the International Association of Outsourcing Professionals (IAOP). The association says the global outsourcing industry is huge, an estimated $6 trillion, based on input from its membership, with more than 150,000 professionals working to manage and support outsource contracts.[9] A Nelson Hall report indicates that much of the growth will come from companies looking to expand their growth and capabilities into emerging markets.[10]

THE RISE OF A TREND: OUTSOURCING FACTS

Economic data for 2006 from the BEA does indicate that outsourcing is on the rise. The BEA's study shows that the share of U.S. gross domestic product (GDP) accounted for by domestic providers of outsourcing services increased to nearly 12, up from 7 percent in 1982.[11] The reason for the rapid growth in outsourcing as a function is clear. As markets develop and competitive pressures escalate, outsourcing continues to be a preferred method of reducing costs and accessing specialist expertise.[12]

This is even truer today as companies work harder than ever to cut costs while trying to maintain and even improve customer service.

For some, outsourcing is highly controversial; however, for many C-level executives, outsourcing has been a strategic weapon capable of significantly improving operational and financial performance as well as increasing shareholder value and driving productivity improvements.[13] Outsourcing has become so commonplace that more than three out of five companies (63 percent) participating in a recent study by the research and consulting firm PricewaterhouseCoopers have outsourced a business process to a third party. Of the 304 top decision makers involved in the study, 46 percent said that outsourcing's importance has increased during the past three years. In addition, 42 percent indicated their company's use of outsourcing has increased. Almost one-quarter (23 percent) have outsourcing programs in their current business plans.

Why is there such an acceptance of outsourcing as a strategy among top executives? Simply put, outsourcing is delivering results! A Deloitte Consulting 2008 Outsourcing Report polled 300 executives who were actively involved with outsourcing services worldwide and found that "83 percent of all respondents reported that their [outsourcing] projects had met their ROI [return on investment] goals of slightly above 25 percent."[14]

A PricewaterhouseCoopers outsourcing study released in 2007 found similar results. In the survey of 293 top global executives, 87 percent said that outsourcing projects delivered the projected benefits, either partially or completely, as defined by the original business case. Thirty-one percent said they "completely" received the projected benefits. Probably the most convincing fact that outsourcing is here to stay is that 91 percent of all respondents said they would outsource again, even if they did not receive the benefits they expected.[15]

TRADITIONAL REASONS FOR OUTSOURCING

What leads companies to outsource? The most common cited reason across the majority of all industries is the need to reduce operating costs. The Deloitte Consulting 2008 Outsourcing Report survey results confirmed that cost reduction is the primary factor motivating most outsourcing decisions by a margin of 64 percent; 49 percent cited the closely related objective of obtaining less expensive labor.[16]

Although cost reduction remains king, the reasons for outsourcing can vary based on business need and industry. Other reasons given for outsourcing are:

- To improve product or service quality
- To mitigate a labor shortage
- To better respond to capacity constraints
- As a catalyst for a major step change that cannot be achieved in house
- To enable the company to focus on core competencies
- To provide seamless 24x7 services or development
- For cost restructuring or converting fixed costs to variable costs
- To reduce time to market by accelerating development or production through the additional capacity
- To reduce risk by transferring some risk to an outsourcer[17]

On complex BPO solutions, improved cash flow is also cited as a key driver for outsourcing. Financial managers recognize that better cash flow represents one of the most attractive benefits of outsourcing because companies are not required to make large up-front investments in assets and business processes (e.g., considerable implementation expenses).[18]

COMMON ISSUES WITH TRADITIONAL OUTSOURCING APPROACHES

With so many companies outsourcing, it is no surprise that many arrangements fail. In the Deloitte survey, 39 percent of the 300 respondents reported that they had terminated at least one outsourcing contract and transferred it to a different vendor, reporting that they were "Dissatisfied" or "Very Dissatisfied" with their largest contract.[19]

The general media is filled with examples of outsourcing deals gone wrong. *Information Week* reported that chief information officers took back 20 percent of offshored IT work in 2006.[20] Yahoo News quoted Marc Lazzari, head of Unisys operations Europe, as stating that he knew of up to 10 deals worth between $890 million and $1.9 billion that were already back on the market despite having been signed less than two years earlier.[21]

But is the future of outsourcing all doom and gloom? Probably one of the best perspectives comes from Michael F. Corbett, chairman of the International Association of Outsourcing Professionals. Corbett confirmed in 2009 that according to IAOP members, 75 percent of organizations reported that they would do the same or more outsourcing in response to the recent financial market crisis and global market downturns. One thing that is not a surprise is that Corbett reports that 19 percent of IAOP members said they have renegotiated prices on existing contracts.[22]

Rather than dwell on the fact that many outsource arrangements are failing, we wanted to dig deeper and look at why. Many studies and articles outlined outsourcing failures; a survey from the Outsourcing Center offers some of the best insights. It found the two biggest reasons outsourcing projects fail is due to unclear expectations and misaligned interests over time.[23]

The Deloitte Consulting 2008 Outsourcing Report validates our premise of misalignment. The survey asked executives what they would do differently if they had to do their outsourcing effort over again. Of the respondents, 49 percent said they would do a better job of defining realistic service levels that are aligned with business goals; 39 percent said they would better define and align business goals with outsourcing strategy.[24]

Unfortunately, most of the outsourcing business models in practice today have inherent flaws in their structure, creating conflict between the company outsourcing and its service provider. This conflict often results in either direct negative behaviors or unconscious behaviors that drive unintended consequences, such as those profiled in chapter 1. As we saw, everyone was working to achieve what was in their own best interest rather than working together for a much broader definition of success.

These inherent flaws in the outsourcing business model are analogous to a virus that spreads throughout the system, leading to a serious ailment. In some cases, the ailment can cause negative side effects, such as metrics that are misreported, underreported, or poorly understood by both parties. Companies or outsource providers in this situation live openly with these infections and often battle the effects on a daily basis, learning how to live with them. In other cases, the ailment lies hidden deep within the relationship, and neither the company outsourcing nor the service provider knows it is there. At first, there may not even be any physical sign, but left unchecked, it may fester into something bigger. In the worst cases, the problem can become so endemic that it eventually causes the death of the relationship, which leads the company to bring the outsourced services back in house or to switch suppliers.

This disruption in an outsourcing arrangement can impact work flow, create distrust and bad will toward customers, and have huge negative effects on the bottom line. It comes down to intrinsic flaws in how companies structure their outsourcing agreements, leading to what is known as perverse incentives. We define a perverse incentive as "An incentive that is intended to promote a desirable effect, but instead creates and nurtures a negative and unintended outcome." In most cases, parties may not even realize there is negative consequence resulting from the incentive.

A classic example of a perverse incentive occurred when the French government instituted a program to eradicate problematic rats in Hanoi, Vietnam, a former possession. The program, initiated in 1902, paid the citizens of Hanoi a bounty for each rat pelt handed in. The program was intended to exterminate rats; instead, it led to the farming of rats.[25]

How does the concept of perverse incentives relate to outsourcing? It is simple, and the examples are numerous. Our research and experience has exposed ten of the most common issues we have seen with outsourcing agreements. We consider these ailments that can plague and potentially destroy an outsourcing relationship. A few are obvious; most are not. One thing in common among all ten is that they drive perverse behaviors and lead to severe strains in the relationship—or, worse, lead to its death.

The next chapter discusses each of these ailments in detail.

CHAPTER 3

TEN AILMENTS OF TRADITIONAL OUTSOURCE RELATIONSHIPS

Nearly all outsourcing arrangements have room for improvement. Outsourcing as a large-scale business practice has not been around long enough to work out all the kinks. Many companies operating with good intentions jumped in without a full understanding of how to outsource correctly. The result: outsourcing deals structured with fundamental flaws in the business model and the relationship. As discussed in chapter 2, the flaws can lead to perverse incentives: direct negative or unconscious behaviors that drive unintended consequences. These perverse incentives lead to 10 common outsourcing ailments we discuss in this chapter.

Read on to discover if your outsource relationship is afflicted by one of these ailments—and then keep reading to find out how to prevent and treat them.

AILMENT 1. PENNY WISE AND POUND FOOLISH

Let us start with the easiest ailment to identify: when a company outsources based purely on costs. We have all heard the warning to not be penny wise and pound foolish. Unfortunately, many procurement professionals still labor in the Dark Ages and have not taken the maxim to heart. Too often companies profess to have an outsource partnership but, behind the scenes, they focus solely on beating up their service providers to get the lowest price.

When outsourcing, think beyond the short-term bottom line. The danger in focusing on the cheapest offer is like anything else—trade-offs are made in quality or service, likely both. Unfortunately, many executives view outsourcing as a quick-fix solution to resolving financial and balance sheet problems. Often companies suffering from a case of penny wise and pound foolish fall into a loop of frequent bidding of their work in a continuous search for a lower -priced provider and then transitioning to that supplier. This can lead to a vicious cycle of bid and transition, bid and transition, bid and transition.

Todd Shire, Logistics Global Sourcing Strategy manager for Intel, commented on how Intel fell into this trap "Our strategy had been to frequently rebid and transition our business from supplier to supplier, always chasing the lowest transaction cost. We could feel comfortable that we were paying the lowest market price for a specific service, but we weren't creating any value through our relationship with our service provider. We were stepping over a dollar to pick up a dime."

When a company gets caught in this cycle, it often ends up with either or both of these unintended consequences:

- Eventually outsource providers will refuse to work with the company again. They get tired of being squeezed on price only to have their efforts rewarded by losing the work to a lower bidder the next time. Ultimately they choose to pursue revenue from more productive outsourcing relationships. In one extreme example, we witnessed a company rebid its transportation services every three months. This company had churned through nearly all of the top 20 suppliers over a five-year period; it was forced to work with suppliers of lesser quality. The result was that the company had several truckloads of its product drive off, never to be seen again.

- Outsource providers sometimes bid so low in order to work with the company that they go out of business, putting the company in a jam to find a new outsource provider. Take, for example, a technology company referred to by suppliers as the 800-Pound Gorilla. This company dabbled with outsourcing its manufacturing and had success. It decided to outsource all of its manufacturing to concentrate on core competencies. Usually this is a smart move. The company's book of business was worth roughly $100 million in revenue for the winning service provider. Three contract manufacturers had the experience and scale to manage the manufacturing volume. The 800-Pound Gorilla went through several rounds of intense negotiations to save the last possible dime on the deal. It awarded the work to a $1 billion outsource provider; the work would provide it with an estimated 10 percent increase in revenue. The problem? The outsource provider essentially "bought" the business but could not sustain the profit losses. It finally gave the 800-Pound Gorilla 30 days' notice that it would no longer manufacture the products and went into bankruptcy, eventually sinking what was once a successful and profitable firm.

Organizations with this ailment give outsourcing a bad name—and should not be outsourcing in the first place. Their myopic focus might pay off in the short term, but time and time again it is proved that it does not pay to be penny wise and pound foolish.

AILMENT 2. THE OUTSOURCING PARADOX

The first symptom manifested by sufferers of ailment 2, the outsourcing paradox, is the development of the "perfect" set of tasks, frequencies, and measures. The "experts" within the company attempt to develop the "perfect" Statement of Work (SOW). Their goal is to tightly define the expected activities. After all, we are taught that we need to clearly define expectations, right? The result is an impressive document containing all the possible details on *how* the work is to be done. At last, the perfect system! However, this "perfect system" is often the first reason why the company will fail in its outsourcing effort. That is because it is the company's perfect system, not one designed by the provider of the services.

Thought leaders in performance-based concepts warn that a poorly written task-frequency specification sometimes can create a harmful and insurmountable obstacle to a successful contract. A too-tightly written Statement of Work makes outsource providers responsible for the work without giving them authority to exercise their own initiative.[1]

We found a classic example of the outsourcing paradox at work in a third-party logistics provider (3PL) that runs a spare parts warehouse. During a site visit, we saw approximately eight people servicing a facility that on average had fewer than 75 orders per day. We asked: Why all the resources? We were told, "That is what the company that is outsourcing requires per our statement of work—so I have staffing at that level to meet the contract requirements."

It is amazing to find that companies have chosen to outsource to the "experts" yet insist on defining the requirements and work scope so tightly that the outsource provider winds up executing the same old inefficient processes! This disease can be exacerbated when coupled with ailment 4, the junkyard dog factor,

AILMENT 3. ACTIVITY TRAP

Many companies that suffer from the outsourcing paradox often also suffer from a related malady, the activity trap. Traditionally, companies that purchase outsourced services use a transaction-based model. Under that model, the service provider is paid for every transaction—whether it is needed or not. Businesses are in the business to make money; outsource providers are no different. The more transactions performed, the more money they make. There is no incentive for the outsource provider to reduce the number of non–value-added transactions, because such a reduction would result in lower revenue.

The activity trap can manifest itself in a variety of transaction-based outsource arrangements. When the contract structure is cost reimbursement, for example, the outsource provider has no incentive to reduce costs because profit is typically a percentage of direct costs. Even if the outsource provider's profit is a fixed amount, the typical company will be penalized for investing in process efficiencies to drive costs down. In a nutshell, the more inefficient the entire support process, the more money the service provider can make. Perverse incentives play a major factor in the activity trap as well. Nineteenth-century paleontologists traveling to China used to pay peasants for each fragment of dinosaur bone (dinosaur fossils) that they produced. They later discovered that peasants dug up the bones and then smashed them to maximize their payments.[2]

Figure 3.1 outlines characteristics of companies suffering from the activity trap in their efforts to outsource third-party logistics services.

Figure 3.1   Activity Trap Characteristics

Company outsourcing for services	Service providers' typical reaction under a transaction-based model
I forecast over.	We charge you to store and count your product monthly...the more you have, the more we make.
I forecast under.	We charge rush fees to expedite your products to market.
I manage my suppliers poorly.	Your suppliers caused us to rework your product into new packaging. We have to charge you more money to rework.
Inventory working capital is killing me.	We don't own your inventory, we just provide services to you. Actually, we like when you have too much because we charge to hold it.
I specified the wrong shipping requirements.	We ship as we are told. You didn't tell us about the special label.
Source: Supply Chain Visions, Ltd.	

Inherent in the activity trap is a disincentive to try to drive down transactions. (This is another symptom seen in the zero-sum game, ailment 7.) But does this really happen? Unfortunately, it does.

On a recent site visit, we asked the general manager of a 3PL what the large area full of orange-tagged pallets was for. She replied, "That's some of our customer's old inventory I need to move to an outside storage facility." When we dug further, we found out it was product that was well over five years old—and at the rate it was moving, it would last 123 years. *(This is not a typo!)* When we pressed further, asking why she did not work with the customer to scrap the material, the answer was "Why? I charge $18 a pallet per month to store it. I'd lose revenue if I did that!"

Another victim of the activity trap, a large technology company, was transferring sales support activities from one outsourced provider to another. It found that the data required to run certain reports was no longer current, and the new data was being stored in a new format in a different location. The current provider had not been made aware of this fact, so the reports that it had produced for the past five months were wrong. In a damage control drill, the service provider learned good news as well as bad news: The sales manager who had requested this reporting had been transferred, and the new sales manager did not use this (now-inaccurate) report. But it was still a required activity, and the technology company was being charged for each report—whether needed or not. Upon further investigation, the company discovered that over 300 unused reports were being generated each month at $75 a report—a whopping $22,500 per month.

A third example of the activity trap comes from outsourced manufacturing. A contract manufacturer performed final kitting and assembly pack-out as a value-added service for an original equipment manufacturer customer that designed consumer electronics. The customer had given the contract manufacturer the bill of materials with detailed instructions to use a specific finished goods "pretty box." This full-color, high-quality box was meant to serve as a kit to hold all of the various components for a particular device, including the manual, cables, charger, and so on. The contractor needed to assemble the box and then insert the parts properly. Making the box required the contractor to have 12 "touches." The contractor charged a flat fee per touch to assemble the box carton, plus a fee of one touch for each item placed in the kit. The contractor knew that the particular box design was not efficient but simply did what it was told rather than suggesting solutions for an improved box design that might eliminate touches.

When outsourcing, is the agreement based on pushing the cash register button every time a specified activity is performed?

AILMENT 4. THE JUNKYARD DOG FACTOR

When the decision to outsource comes down, it means jobs likely will be lost as the work and jobs transition to the outsource provider. The result? Often employees will go to great lengths to hunker down and stake territorial claims to certain processes that simply "must" stay in house. We call this ailment the junkyard dog factor. Even if the majority of the jobs are outsourced, many companies choose to have their "best" employees stay on board to manage the new outsource provider. These same "best" employees are often the ones who were asked to help write the Statement of Work. Is it any wonder that SOWs can become such rigid documents of often-less-than-optimal ways the company was performing the tasks that are now being outsourced? The result: misaligned desired outcomes. The company gets what it contracted for—but it is not really what it wanted. Over time, this ailment affects the outsource provider as well. Under a transaction-based model, the service provider is rewarded for work associated with the volume of the transactions. Unless otherwise compensated, the last thing an outsource provider wants to do is develop process efficiencies that eliminate its own revenue. So a company that might begin outsourcing to find an efficient and low-cost *total solution* instead achieves the lowest cost for an activity without really achieving its desired outcomes. This discourages innovation, at the company outsourcing and also at the outsource provider. The junkyard dog factor often results in inefficient and overbuilt infrastructure, because each touch point in the process has tried to optimize its individual part either to keep jobs or to earn revenue associated with tasks.

One common example of how the junkyard dog factor leads to overbuilt infrastructure occurs when a function is outsourced and the company keeps on far too many individuals that performed the function internally to become "supplier managers". The net effect is a duplication of overhead and over-proscriptive process management. When a company outsources, they should reinvest internal resources in higher value activities. If they don't do that, then the outsourced solution doesn't live up to its value and the business case is unrealized.

AILMENT 5. THE HONEYMOON EFFECT

At the beginning of any relationship, both parties go through the honeymoon stage. The Stamford, Connecticut, research firm Gartner, Inc. studied the honeymoon effect and found that overall attitudes toward an outsourcing contract tend to be positive at the outset, but satisfaction levels drop over time.[3] Outsource providers often jump through hoops as they ramp up and begin to collect revenue from their new client.

Although it remains conscientious about meeting the company's expectations and associated service levels outlined in the contract, under typical arrangements, the service provider does not have an inherent incentive to raise service levels (or decrease the price), even if industry service levels are improving. Over time, the downside of the honeymoon effect can lead directly to the famed Seven-Year Itch: The supplier's productivity levels may begin to decline if it is not investing in its people and technology. Then the outsourcing company, feeling dissatisfied with the supplier's service levels and productivity, will want to switch to a new supplier. However, suppliers can make it costly and disruptive for owners to exercise this right.[4]

AILMENT 6. SANDBAGGING

To prevent the honeymoon effect, some companies have adopted approaches to encourage outsource providers to perform better over time by establishing bonus payments for them to achieve certain levels of performance. This can work, but unfortunately, and all too often, it creates perverse incentives for the outsource provider, whereby the company achieves just the amount of improvement needed to get the incentive. Consider Ukrainian Sergey Bubka, who was a world-class pole-vaulter earning up to $50,000 every time he set a new world record. From 1983 to 1998 he set world records 35 times...but never by more than one centimeter![5]

Let us look at a typical outsourcing example of sandbagging. Many times during contract negotiation someone on the company side, frequently senior management, will ask, "Just how much *can* I save?" Rather than establish the highest level of savings achievable as early as possible, which would be most beneficial to the company outsourcing, the outsource provider sandbags and offers up the savings in smaller increments over time. The same is true with service improvements. Why deliver it all up front when your hardnosed customer is just going to hammer you for more next quarter or next year? Companies know that the savings are made up of low-hanging fruit and long-term savings. They often hold back some of their short-term improvements in an effort to manufacture savings opportunities down the line, in case they do not perform in future quarters or years.

AILMENT 7. THE ZERO-SUM GAME

One of the most common ailments afflicting outsourcing arrangements is the zero-sum game; outsourcing companies play this game when they believe, mistakenly, that if something is good for the outsource provider, then it is automatically bad for them. Outsource providers also play this game. Players on each side do not understand that the sum of the parts *can* actually be better when they are combined effectively, which was proven by John Nash's Nobel Prize–winning research in the area of game theory. The basic premise of Nash's game theory is that when individuals or organizations play a game together and work together to solve a problem, the results are *always* better than if they had worked separately or played against each other.

We have all played games in business school and simulations that prove this concept (the supply chain beer game, the astronaut on the moon game, etc.). The first step in overcoming this ailment is to recognize that an outsourcing relationship should actively seek win-win solutions. Unfortunately, customers of many outsource providers that try to cure this condition often are suffering from the activity trap or the outsource paradox. Although the outsource providers want to be proactive, the contract's pricing model provides incentives to perform non-value-added activities for their customers. Or worse, companies that outsource display the Junkyard Dog factor and do not value the outsource providers' innovative ideas.

AILMENT 8. DRIVING BLIND DISEASE

Another aliment that bedevils many outsourcing agreements is the driving blind disease: the lack of a formal governance process to monitor the performance of the relationship. When we started working with companies more than 20 years ago, most outsourcing arrangements fell into this trap. It was very common to find multi-million dollar outsourcing contracts that did not outline how the companies would measure their success. Typically the companies would track costs but not measure various aspects of performance. As a result, early outsourcing agreements often failed because of an unclear definition of success.

According to the Aberdeen Group, a research firm, ensuring that negotiated savings actually are realized on the bottom line is one of the biggest challenges facing organizations today. The term *savings leakage* is used to refer to the difference between the savings that were identified and the actual savings that were achieved.[6]

According to Todd Shire of Intel,

When we recalculate the ROI [return on investment] of an outsourcing agreement after implementation and stabilization, we sometimes find that anticipated savings were not realized because we needed to change scope or pricing in order to meet service expectations. When this happens, there is often devastating damage done to the customer/service provider relationship that stops all potential progress towards mutual value creation. If we had agreed with the supplier on specific outcomes like service levels instead of transactions and headcount, the 'leakage' could have been avoided.

Proper measurement and follow-up of the key cost drivers is critical to preventing this leakage. In addition, leaders in this area have linked incentives to total cost savings *achieved* versus initial savings negotiated. Other companies have secured support from company leadership to align sourcing and spend compliance with corporate goals and incentives.[7]

The good news is that in the past five years, we have seen numerous firms—both companies that outsource and outsource providers—putting in place scorecards or dashboards to measure how outsource providers are performing. Dashboards provide a feedback loop that helps the organization involved get data on how it is doing. It is important to understand that using a scorecard alone will not solve all of your problems. But if you do not have one, think about getting one now. However, keep in mind that using a dashboard improperly can result in one or both of the next two ailments.

AILMENT 9. MEASUREMENT MINUTIAE

Most of us probably remember Mom's warning that too much of a good thing can be bad for you, perhaps while you were gobbling up your Halloween candy. The same concept applies to measurement of outsource providers. The hallmark of measurement minutiae is trying to measure *everything*. It is remarkable the minutiae that some organizations are able to create. We have found spreadsheets with 50 to 100 metrics on them. Measurement minutiae often is associated with companies that also are suffering from the junkyard dog factor and agreements that are typified by the activity trap.

One company we visited had so many metrics that it needed a binder to keep track of everything on a monthly basis. Managers were embarrassed to tell us the total person-hours across all the organizations required to create these spreadsheets. Now, this is not a wasted effort if the company is getting positive results based on improvements it is making. Unfortunately, our experience has shown that few companies have the diligence to actively manage all of the metrics they have created.

AILMENT 10. THE POWER OF NOT DOING

The saddest of all ailments is the one we call the power of not doing. We recently observed a case of this ailment at a Fortune 50 company. A senior manager was demonstrating what a great job her company had done on establishing measures. It had signed up for a seminar to learn how to apply the Balanced Scorecard and had hired a consulting firm to help create a world-class scorecard. The company had invested more than $1 million in an automated scorecard solution to capture and graph performance. Each of the supplier scorecards was posted on an internal Web site. One could quickly click through to look at the current measures and performance.

As this manager pulled up a scorecard, we randomly pointed to a measure and said, "This metric seems to be in the red. [The scorecards were color coded; red indicated poor performance.] When was the last time your team discussed this performance with the outsource provider?" The response? She looked us straight in the eye and answered honestly that she had no idea. She knew they had quarterly business reviews with their "top" suppliers, but the dashboard in question was not for one of these suppliers. We went on to ask, "How rigorously do you adhere to quarterly business reviews?" She was embarrassed to say that they were lucky if they met with their suppliers once or twice a year.

This case of the power of not doing is not unusual—many companies have fallen into the trap of establishing measures for the sake of measures and have not thought through how they will be used to manage the business. We have all heard the old adage "You can't manage what you don't measure," but if the metrics compiled are not used to make adjustments and improvements, do not expect results.

A variation on this ailment—harking back to penny wise and pound foolish—involves activities that the service provider does not perform, usually linked to common perverse incentives. For example, consider that fire departments often are funded according to the number of fire calls made. Obviously, this is intended to reward fire departments that do the most work. However, it may discourage them from fire-prevention activities, which are not measured or compensated.[8]

Then there is the practice of paying medical professionals and reimbursing insured patients for treatment but not for prevention—which discourages early discovery and increases total costs.[9]

These ailments and any combination of them can be found in many outsourcing arrangements. By identifying the problems, we can develop solutions. Chapter 4 walks you through the changes that companies need to make to improve both outsourcing arrangements and, most important, performance.

PART II

SETTING THE RULES

CHANGING THE GAME: THE RISE OF VESTED OUTSOURCING

Is there a better way?

Can companies develop an outsourcing model that prevents the ten ailments outlined in chapter 3?

These are the questions that Todd Shire, Global Logistics Sourcing Strategy manager for Intel, asked when he contacted the University of Tennessee after hearing about its program and outsourcing research.

"We were exploring possible solutions for improving how we outsourced when we came across the university's original research and we realized that we didn't need to reinvent the wheel; that there were concepts we could immediately apply. I contacted them even before I even finished the first page."

At Intel, outsourcing is big business. It had come to rely on outsource service providers across many areas of its business. When Shire first started to work in the logistics group, he began reviewing the nearly 100 different outsourced services Intel had worldwide. Todd explained Intel's dilemma, which is typical of the classic zero-sum game ailment outlined in chapter 3.

> In order to get to the next level for some of our logistics business, we needed to do things differently with our supply base. We had come to realize over time that our approach of frequently bidding our suppliers to chase the best market price was inhibiting innovation—and innovation is a big deal at Intel. Our

suppliers were reluctant to invest in innovation or to propose new processes because of the risk that we will bid their business out and potentially take it away. They simply could not justify an investment in innovation or collaboration because they may not realize the ROI [return on investment]. And many were asserting that Intel was leaving money on the table through overmanagement and by dictating processes.

Unfortunately, although companies generally want to improve their outsourcing practices, most are not sure where to begin and how to make systematic changes.

The University of Tennessee has been researching this challenge for four years and has taken the lessons learned to create a systematic model to improve outsourcing as a business practice. We call this model Vested Outsourcing because the core principle is to create an outsourcing relationship where companies and their suppliers become vested in each other's success, creating a true win-win solution. This chapter shares the key findings of our research, which we have distilled into five key rules. When applied to a business practice, these rules will improve outsourcing relationships, increase innovation, and improve efficiency. Further, by following these rules, you can determine whether Vested Outsourcing is the appropriate approach to take for a particular service.

PRIMER ON TYPES OF SOURCING RELATIONSHIPS

Traditionally, most procurement professionals and textbooks outline three types of sourcing models, whether a firm is buying a commodity such as furniture or a service such as call center operations. These three sourcing models are:

1. Transactional. The supplier is effectively kept at arm's length, and a purchase order is issued for every transaction. This is typical when transactions are infrequent, low cost, or have little impact on the firm. For instance, an office may use a caterer for an annual employee banquet. The supplier is not strategic or critical to the operation of the firm.

2. Preferred Supplier. This supplier is prequalified, either through a firm's formal certification process or informally by having a positive track record of proven experience. A preferred supplier often is granted certain procedures, such as blanket purchase orders. Northrop Grumman Electronic Systems developed a Preferred Supplier Program to identify and recognize high-performing, best-in-class suppliers that support the firm's core products. By developing the program, Northrop Grumman ensured increases in performance and operational efficiency at its and the supplier's facility in the areas of technical requirements, cost, schedule and delivery, and quality.[1]

3. Strategic Alliance. This link is characterized by a C-level relationship between two companies with shared intelligence and operational tie-ins. These relationships are efforts to meet a business need while still remaining separate firms and often require the strategic interweaving of infrastructure. Apple's iPhone voice mail application, developed along with AT&T, is an example of two firms with such a relationship. Best Buy and TiVo have also announced an alliance that they say will "transform the digital home entertainment experience." Both firms plan to investigate the development of a unique user interface for TiVo digital video recorders purchased at Best Buy, which would allow the store to better market its digital content services and store offers.[2]

Vested Outsourcing partnerships create a new relationship category that lies between preferred suppliers and strategic alliances. The relationship is more focused than the strategic alliance and does not require as much operational infrastructure. It takes the preferred supplier relationship to a new level (see Figure 4.1).

Figure 4.1   Supplier Relationships

No two Vested Outsourcing partnerships are alike, but the good ones achieve a new level of success based on optimizing three key goals—what we call the performance pyramid:

1. Innovation and improved service
2. Reducing cost to the company outsourcing
3. Improving profits to the outsource provider (see Figure 4.2)

Conventional wisdom says that there is typically a trade-off among these three goals. For example, achieving higher service levels often costs more money. Allowing the service provider to double its profit margin may raise the cost for the company that is outsourcing.

A theme we saw in our research was that progressive companies have been reinventing their outsourcing practices. They and their service providers work together to develop performance-based solutions where both parties' interests are aligned so that they both receive tangible benefits.[3] Thus, they are vested in each other's success by creating ways to optimize for the three goals where conventionally they are viewed as requiring a trade-off.

The heart of a Vested Outsourcing contract is an agreement based on desired outcomes that explicitly states the results on which the companies will base the outsource contract. A desired outcome is defined as a *measurable objective* that focuses on what will be accomplished as a result

Figure 4.2   Performance Pyramid

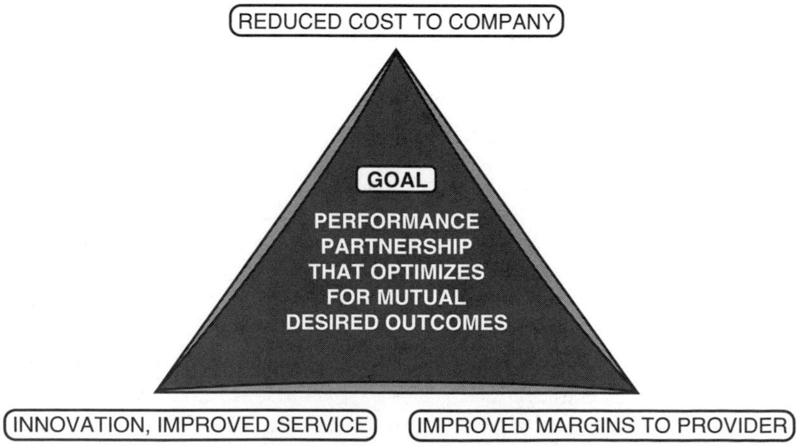

of the work performed. To be effective, desired outcomes must have supporting metrics that objectively indicate whether the outcome has been accomplished or not.

For instance, suppose an individual had as a desired outcome to get in shape. It would be critical to understand the motivating factor behind that desire and the metrics that would be used to define success. Is it simply defined as weight loss? Or the ability to run a marathon? Or to impress others with bigger biceps? Or the need to reduce the risk of heart disease? Once it is clear what get in shape means, the next step is to select metrics that can be used to clearly define what is success. Let us explore some easy-to-understand examples to get a clear picture of what we mean when we use the term *desired outcomes.*

- 5-foot 1-inch 50-year-old woman: Improve overall health by losing 40 pounds and achieve a body mass index of 25.
- 39-year-old woman: Complete a marathon in three hours or less to demonstrate she is not getting old.
- 20-year-old man: Bench-press 225 pounds for 18 repetitions in order to develop large muscles that will impress young women.
- 65-year-old heart attack victim: Reduce the risk of future heart attacks by reducing cholesterol levels to less than 200, reducing blood pressure to 130/80, and quit smoking within three months.

In each of these examples, there is a motive carefully linked to one or more measures and targets that, when achieved, will clearly define success for each person. While achieving any of these metrics could be used to get in shape, the definitions vary greatly so we need to be specific about our goals as they relate to our motives.

In a business setting, a Vested Outsourcing agreement clearly defines the motives, associated metrics, and targets that are desired. In addition, financial rewards and/or penalties are set for not meeting or for exceeding agreed-on desired outcomes. In such an agreement, regardless of what is being outsourced, the partner has the ability to earn additional financial value—more profit—by contractually committing to achieve the desired outcomes. Simply stated: If the outsource provider achieves the desired results, it receives incentive payments that boost its profitability.

It is important to understand that Vested Outsourcing is *not* gain-sharing. Gainsharing is a concept that shares cost savings; it is usually structured to share a portion of cost savings between the parties in the outsourcing agreement. Gainsharing typically is based on productivity measures and on reducing the cost of service for a specified range of activities. Vested Outsourcing is much broader than gainsharing because it includes not only the cost-reduction concepts from gainsharing, it also includes increases in revenue, benefits received from service-level improvements, inventory reductions, or process improvements, to name a few. How Vested Outsourcing agreements work is detailed later.

Microsoft has started down the path of Vested Outsourcing. It has always been an advocate for outsourcing noncore activities; however, more recently, Bill Gates has stated that outsourcing even mission-critical work offshore is now a "common sense proposition."[4]

One service that Microsoft has long outsourced is its facilities management services. Microsoft operates in over 100 buildings on five different campuses covering approximately 10 million square feet; maintaining those campuses is a huge expense.[5] Microsoft wanted to drive deep cost improvements in facilities management, but it feared that beating up service providers with regard to price might have a negative effect on their service levels. Poor service levels likely would irritate their employees or, even worse, result in safety, security, or environmental compliance issues. Microsoft teamed with the facilities management consulting boutique firm Expense Management Solutions, Inc. to create a Vested Outsourcing relationship, which Microsoft referred to as its Third Generation Outsourcing Model. Three key strategies of Microsoft's outsourcing relationship were transparency of costs, placing a percentage of the supplier's fee at risk, and creating a shared incentive program for reducing overall costs.

The first element of the strategy was to leverage a cost-plus pricing model. (Pricing models are described in detail in chapter 9.) This model allowed Microsoft to have transparency on its real costs. Transparency was important because one of Microsoft's primary desired outcomes was to reduce its total spend on facilities management, and the lion's share of the expense was in actual maintenance costs, not in the fees charged by their service provider.

Although a cost-plus pricing model helped Microsoft gain cost transparency, it did not encourage its suppliers to reduce costs, especially if there were tough service-level standards to meet. In fact, as stated in chapter 3, a cost-plus pricing model often leads to the activity trap ailment because the service provider actually would lose revenue if it were to reduce costs. Cost-plus providers sometimes are pressured to overstaff in order to ensure that high service levels are consistently met. For these reasons, Microsoft and its supplier—Grubb & Ellis—agreed on two other strategies that would help foster high service levels *and* overall cost reductions while preserving profit margins for Grubb & Ellis.

The second strategy Microsoft and Grubb & Ellis agreed on was placing a portion of Grubb & Ellis' fee for managing the business (its profit) at risk. Under this strategy, Grubb & Ellis would earn its full profit margins by achieving specific predefined and measurable service levels. For example, if Grubb & Ellis typically had a 10 percent profit margin, the Vested Outsourcing agreement included a reduced margin to manage Microsoft's facilities. Put another way, Grubb & Ellis placed a portion of its margin at risk if it was not able to meet Microsoft's service levels. Microsoft's intention was for Grubb & Ellis to receive 100 percent of the at-risk fee; not obtaining that fee was seen as an operational shortcoming that needed to be fixed, not as a savings for Microsoft.

The last strategy implemented was to create a cost-saving incentive for Grubb & Ellis to drive Microsoft's overall costs down. As stated earlier, this cost-saving incentive often is referred to as gainsharing. Grubb & Ellis received a portion of every $1 in costs that it was able to help Microsoft save in its facilities management budget. The better Grubb & Ellis was at driving Microsoft's costs down, the more money it would make and the fewer costs Microsoft would have. Grubb & Ellis was actively encouraged and financially motivated to invest its own money in process improvements that would drive down costs for Microsoft.

The result? A Vested Outsourcing relationship that created a true win-win outsourcing relationship that optimized for service-level performance, cost reduction, and Grubb & Ellis margin improvements. After only the first two years the program was in place, Microsoft and Grubb & Ellis achieved these service-level improvements:

- The gap between Microsoft expectations and supplier performance decreased more than 91 percent.
- 22 percent savings based on a cost-plus fee at-risk pricing model.

- 9 percent additional savings as a result of the collaborative efforts of each company under the cost-sharing provision of the contract.[6]
- Improvement in Grubb & Ellis profit margin.

In fact, the relationship was so successful that Grubb & Ellis won Microsoft's coveted Supplier of the Year award in 2007 and Microsoft's Environmental Supplier of the Year award in 2008 for its innovation in environmental sustainability.

Under a Vested Outsourcing dynamic, the outsource provider is challenged to apply brainpower and possibly financial investments to address the company's needs. It also takes on the risk, in essence putting skin in the game. The outsource provider looks at how it can best apply the right processes, technologies, and capabilities that will drive value to the company that is outsourcing. The outsource provider's commitment to deliver against projected value for the company outsourcing, such as a commitment to reduce costs or improve service or both, shifts risk to the outsource provider. In exchange, the company doing the outsourcing commits to allow the outsource provider to earn additional profit above and beyond the industry average for its service area for achieving this incremental value. The result is a win-win vested outsourcing partnership: a paradigm shift explored in the next section.

MIND-SHIFT CHANGE OF VESTED OUTSOURCING

It is important to understand that Vested Outsourcing is much more than delivering a higher level of service on a given activity. For example, it is:

- NOT about achieving 99 percent fill rate for your warehouse provider versus 95 percent.
- NOT about answering 95 percent of all calls in 20 seconds versus 30 seconds.
- NOT about reducing quality defects from 3,000 defective parts per million (DPPM) to Six Sigma quality levels of 3.4 DPPM from the contract manufacturer.
- NOT about ensuring that the janitorial service provider cleans the toilets every 2 hours.

Unfortunately, in a Vested Outsourcing relationship, many people are not exposed to the elements that comprise its fundamental business model concepts. Yet the whole of this arrangement is far greater than the sum of its parts. A common mistake occurs when an organization believes it has a Vested Outsourcing agreement because it has taken an existing contract and simply added a single component of Vested Outsourcing. That would be like thinking that adding a BMW logo to a Honda Insight will make the Honda faster. *Vested Outsourcing is a fundamental business model paradigm shift in how the outsourcing company and its service providers work together.* The heart of a Vested Outsourcing agreement is a true win-win relationship between the outsourcing company and its outsource provider.

WIIFWe versus WIIFM

Many organizations boast that they have solid partnerships in place, but our experience and research has found that most of them really want to enhance and push their own self-interest. This is often known as a what's-in-it-for-me (WIIFM) approach. Such an attitude is understandable because winning is ingrained from early childhood on; indeed, most institutions of higher education also focus on winning. In fact, many organizations formally train procurement and sales professionals in the art of negotiation to help them win.

The word *partner* implies that there are not two sides. Progressing toward a Vested Outsourcing agreement should focus on creating a culture where parties are working together to ensure their ultimate success. There is a significant difference between being a supplier and being a partner. The mentality should shift from an us versus them to a we philosophy, as discussed earlier in avoiding the zero-sum game. We call this a what's-in-it-for-we (WIIFWe) philosophy. Vested Outsourcing is indeed a true partnership.

Companies should approach a Vested Outsourcing agreement as a symbiotic relationship because only by working together can everyone succeed. A Vested Outsourcing partnership focuses on identifying desired outcomes and then aligns the interests of all players so that all benefit if the desired outcomes are reached. The relationship becomes more collaborative and expands beyond simply meeting the requirements of the original outsourcing agreement.

A Bigger Pie is Better

A WIIFWe philosophy strives to increase the size of the entire pie by unlocking a greater opportunity than currently is realized by either party rather than by maximizing the size of the slice for any one player, such as lower costs at the expense of the outsource provider's profits. WIIFWe tosses the conventional win/lose mentality out the window. A company that is trying to maximize its piece of the pie instead of growing the whole pie is not playing under Vested Outsourcing rules and most likely will craft an outsourcing agreement that contains one or more of the ailments outlined in chapter 3.

Many may think that a win-win approach is too idealistic. Is it really possible? For instance, earlier we discussed the contract manufacturer that had to touch a box 12 times to assemble the package. Under a Vested Outsourcing partnership, that supplier would have substantial incentives to help the customer redesign the packaging to reduce the total cost. Let us say that the supplier helped design a box that cost 2 cents more to manufacture but reduced the number of touches from 12 to 7. If the touches cost 2 cents each, and the annual quantity is 5 million pieces, the annual net savings would be $400,000. Wouldn't any customer be willing to share that with the supplier?

Why would a supplier suggest a change like this, one that reduces revenue? After all, the goal is to make as much money as possible, and cutting the revenue stream does not seem a way to accomplish this goal. However, if suppliers are rewarded for innovative thinking to drive efficiencies, they are more apt to achieve their clients' desired outcomes even when it means their revenue will decline. In essence, suppliers are rewarded for applying their brainpower, not just paid for executing an activity.

In addition, reducing costs for a client can lead to more business, more locations, new services, referrals, and the ability to leverage the lessons from the experience across the organization to become more efficient.

Consider the discount airline JetBlue. In an effort to bring humanity back to air travel, the company decided to outsource the things that do not touch customers. As a result, it entered into a ten-year agreement with MTU Aero Engines to do heavy maintenance on the jet engines. JetBlue was able to reduce its maintenance risk due to unforeseen repairs and to develop a more predictable cost, as maintenance fees were determined by such factors as flight hours, engine type, and age.

MTU benefited by knowing it had a predictable volume of maintenance over a decade, and could invest in training, equipment, and processes that would yield a return over the life of the contract.

Was it a good deal? Within 18 months of signing the original contract, JetBlue and MTU inked a five-year extension.

Developing a WIIFWe relationship is easier to describe than to implement. Evolving from a culture of oversight and control to one of mutual respect is a difficult transition for most companies. Adversarial relationships often persist, and getting to a true win-win relationship can take time and practice. We frequently suggest assigning a neutral party to the team, much like a golf pro or a tennis coach, to act as the win-lose coach to point out when organizations slip into conventional win-lose thinking.

Vested Outsourcing is not for the faint of heart; it challenges the mind-set of senior executives, middle managers, and especially procurement specialists. It often requires the willpower to walk away from an immediate price savings gained from procurement muscle in order to save more money in the future. Last, it requires committed executive leadership from each organization. The need for senior management support is true for every major business improvement, whether it is total quality management, reengineering, or Lean. Unfortunately, many senior executives have reached that position because of their adherence to a conventional approach to outsourcing, and they may be unwilling to change their business style. Vested Outsourcing demands a willingness to transcend the conventional win-lose approach most companies take in procuring goods and services.

Without this mind-set and cultural shift, Vested Outsourcing will not work. The good news? The outsourcing agreement and your partnership likely will be better than a strictly conventional approach, because you have at least explored the limits and expectations of the relationship. Simply going through the process allows everyone involved to have a clearer understanding of the expectations. While you might not be able to go the whole nine yards to create a fully Vested Outsourcing agreement, you likely will be able to avoid at least some of the typical outsource ailments.

Even when there is commitment at the most senior levels in the organizations, middle-level managers can succumb to ailment 4, the junkyard dog factor. That is, employees will go to great lengths to stake their territorial claim to certain processes that they insist must stay in house to protect themselves and their turf. This ailment can afflict some companies so severely that they have to remove employees to get beyond that conventional win-lose thinking.

The culture of adversarial relationships is rampant in the legal profession, obviously, as well as in the approach of some contracting professionals. It is critical that companies creating a Vested Outsourcing agreement ensure their legal and procurement teams fully understand the need to move away from adversarial relationships and to stress the benefit of win-win over the long haul. The win-lose coach can come in handy in keeping the contract and legal departments in check. If people's behavior presents an obstacle, whenever possible, they should be removed and replaced with managers open to forging a win-win attitude.

A true win-win requires effort and commitment by all parties. Outsourcing does not mean abdication: It must be a partnership with regular, frequent communication to manage the expectations as well as the work. Although the most pernicious problems that affect outsource arrangements usually are brought on by micromanagement, a different set of problems can emerge when a company hands over a process or multiple processes completely to the outsource provider.

Human relationships are fundamental to successful Vested Outsourcing. Almost by definition, effective partnerships must evolve over time as the parties learn to operate under a win-win philosophy. For many companies, this approach is a learned behavior, and they have to unlearn conventional patterns and ways of thinking. Without mutual trust, any attempt to implement Vested Outsourcing will become mired in terms and conditions. In addition, the outsourcing company and the outsource provider need to make sure they are comfortable in their new roles. The company outsourcing needs to feel comfortable describing the "what" and delegating the "how" to the outsource provider. The outsource provider must be comfortable signing up to take the risk to deliver the "how." Organizations constantly must seek to overcome roadblocks in the processes, infrastructure, technology, and people that prevent mutual success.

Most companies that use a Vested Outsourcing approach do not spend much time talking about how it gives their service providers the opportunity to make more money. They focus instead on how it delivers better value or better performance at the same or lower total cost. Nevertheless, service providers that work under Vested Outsourcing partnerships often focus on its higher profit potential and point to the fact that successfully designed Vested Outsourcing partnerships create happier clients. Because both organizations are working together to achieve a common set of results, Vested Outsourcing does work based on the mutual-relationship philosophy, which is what partnership is all about. Each organization may have different motivations, but both share the same set of desired outcomes. They are vested in each other's success.

In our experience, only those organizations that truly challenge the conventional WIIFM mentality are able to achieve true Vested Outsourcing partnerships that deliver outstanding results. Adopting anything less that WIIFWe philosophy will result in less-than-optimal results.

FIVE RULES OF VESTED OUTSOURCING

Deeply wedded to the WIIFWe philosophy are the Five Rules, shown below and in Figure 4.3:

1. Focus on outcomes, not transactions.
2. Focus on the WHAT, not the HOW.
3. Agree on clearly defined and measurable outcomes.
4. Optimize pricing model incentives for cost/service trade-offs.
5. Governance structure provides insight, not merely oversight.

Figure 4.3   The Five Rules of Vested Outsourcing

Rule #1: Focus on Outcomes, Not Transactions

Many conventional outsourcing arrangements are built around a transactional model (as noted in ailment 3, the activity trap, from chapter 3). Most often this transaction-based model is coupled with a cost-plus or a competitively bid fixed-price-per-transaction pricing model to ensure the company buying the services is getting the lowest cost *per transaction*. The service provider is paid for every transaction— whether it is needed or not. Thus, the more inefficient the entire process, the more money the service provider can make.

This model achieves the lowest cost for transactions for the company outsourcing but often does not help the company achieve what it really wants or needs. The company that has outsourced gets what it contracted, but perhaps that is not the best solution. Vested Outsourcing operates under a desired outcome-based model, with the emphasis on having the outsource provider align its interests to what the company really wants: an efficient and low-cost total support solution.

A Vested Outsourcing business model fundamentally shifts how a company buys services in a performance-based approach. The concept of Vested Outsourcing is fairly straightforward; instead of paying an outsource provider for unit transactions for various service activities, such as warehousing, transportation, spare parts, repairs, or hours of technical support, the company and its service provider agree on desired outcomes. Desired outcomes are still quantifiable but take a different form: they can be set availability, reliability, cost, revenue generation, employee or customer satisfaction, or even asset investment targets. In essence, *Vested Outsourcing buys desired outcomes, not individual transactions*. The service provider is paid based on its ability to achieve the mutually agreed desired outcomes.

Rule #2: Focus on the WHAT, Not the HOW

Adopting a Vested Outsourcing business model does not change the nature of the work to be performed. At the operational level, there is still a need for lines of code to be written, bathrooms to be cleaned, orders to be fulfilled, spares and repairs to be managed, calls to be answered. and meals to be cooked. What does change is the way that the outsourcing company purchases the services.

Using Vested Outsourcing, the company outsourcing specifies what it wants and moves the responsibility of determining how it gets delivered to the outsource provider. According to the outsourcing paradox, firms outsource to a supplier because they know the supplier can do a better job, yet write the contract as if they are the experts. Good companies outsource for a reason: in-house operations are either too expensive, ineffective, or both.

The most effective Vested Outsourcing partnerships include minimal discussion of the processes the service providers will follow to meet the requirements; they focus instead on system-wide performance expectations. Why dictate in an area where you have decided you are deficient? It is up to the service providers to understand how to put the supporting processes together to achieve the desired outcomes.

Consider information technology outsourcing arrangements. Under a conventional contract, the company outsourcing would specify the hardware to use and possibly even the number and skills of help desk personnel. This scenario diminishes the outsource provider's role as the expert. The service provider is the one that is constantly in the marketplace and keeping tabs on the latest developments. Its experts certainly will know of the most appropriate hardware for a given task, and they may even know of process or system efficiencies that allow them to do the task with less labor than non-IT firms. *Performance partnerships let each firm do what it does best.* Unless the company that is outsourcing has the skills and the resources to keep up with the latest innovations in the service it is outsourcing, it should leave the details to the experts.

Depending on the scope of the partnership, the company that is outsourcing transfers some or all of the activities that need to be performed to achieve the contract goals to the service provider. For example, when outsourcing cleaning services, a company could outsource all aspects of maintaining restroom facilities, which might expand the outsource provider's scope to include managing plumbing needs or procuring supplies.

Collaboration lies at the heart of Vested Outsourcing because, to be successful, often a service provider becomes responsible for more services and has to work with other service providers. In a properly constructed Vested Outsourcing partnership, the service provider no longer has the option to throw up its hands and say "Not my fault!" Rule #4 (optimize pricing model incentives for cost/service trade-offs) works in conjunction with this rule to create the positive forces to prevent the blame game.

Rule #3: Agree on Clearly Defined and Measurable Outcomes

The third hallmark of a good Vested Outsourcing partnership is clearly defined and measurable desired outcomes, which are essential to avoid ailment 8, driving blind. All parties must be explicit in defining the outcomes they want. These outcomes are expressed in terms of a limited set—ideally, no more than five—high-level metrics. Organizations should spend the time, collaboratively, during the outsourcing process, and especially during contract negotiations, to establish explicit definitions for how relationship success will be measured. Investing time up front is critical to ensure that none of the companies spends time or resources after implementation measuring the wrong things.

Once the desired outcomes are agreed on and explicitly defined, the service provider can propose a solution that will deliver the required level of performance at a predetermined price. This approach fundamentally shifts the business model, shifting risk from the company that is outsourcing to the service provider(s). Under the purest form of Vested Outsourcing, the company that is outsourcing pays only for results, not transactions; rather than being paid for the activity performed, service providers are paid for the value delivered by their overall solution.

It is vital to get this right. Getting it wrong can result in hundreds of thousands, and possibly millions, of dollars wasted in an outsource solution that is plagued by the ailments described in chapter 3. The company will have procured a solution that gets what it asked for but may not necessarily be what it wants. Also, take care to avoid ailment 9, measurement minutiae. Too much of a good thing is still bad!

Rule #4: Optimize Pricing Model Incentives for Cost/Service Trade-offs

The fourth hallmark of a Vested Outsourcing partnership is a properly structured pricing model that incorporates incentives for the best cost and service trade-off. This is essential to avoid ailment 1, penny wise and pound foolish. The pricing model is based on the type of contract—fixed price or cost reimbursement—that will be used to reward the outsource provider.

When establishing the pricing model, businesses should apply two principles:

1. The pricing model must balance risk and reward for the organizations. The agreement should be structured to ensure that the outsource provider assumes risk only for decisions within its control. For example, a transportation service provider should never be penalized for the rising costs of fuel, and a property management service provider should never be penalized for an increase in energy prices.

2. The agreement should specify that the service provider will deliver solutions, not just activities. When properly constructed, Vested Outsourcing will provide incentives to the service provider to solve the customer's problems. The better the service provider is at solving those problems, the more profits the service provider can make. Outsource providers are thus encouraged to develop and institute innovative and cost-effective methods of performing work to drive down total cost while maintaining or improving service.

The essence of Vested Outsourcing is a strategic bet by the outsource provider that it will meet the service levels at the agreed price. Inherent in the business model is a reward for the service provider to make investments in process, service, or associated product that will generate returns in excess of contract requirements. Performance partnerships usually are based around achieving the desired trade-off stated by achieving:

• Higher service levels at the same cost
• The same service levels at lower costs
• Higher service levels *and* lower costs

If the service provider does a good job, it will reap the rewards of greater profitability.

Vested Outsourcing does *not* guarantee higher profits for service providers, but it does provide them with the authority and autonomy to make strategic investments in their processes and product reliability that can generate a greater return on investment than a conventional cost-plus or fixed-price-per-transaction contract might yield. Vested Outsourcing also typically seeks to encourage service providers to meet the desired performance levels at a flat or decreasing cost over time. Therefore, the service provider has to leverage its unique skills and capabilities to make the processes more efficient—to the point that it can generate increased profit. By doing so, the outsource provider may earn intangible benefits, such as contract extensions, additional business or locations, expanded services to provide to the partner, or the willingness of the customer to provide references.

Vested Outsourcing arrangements should be based on reducing the *total cost* of the process being outsourced—not simply the budget for the outsourced services. The interwoven dependencies of outsourcing relationships require an environment that encourages service providers to push outsourcing companies to change internal processes if they are inhibiting the success of Vested Outsourcing. Outsourcing companies also must be open-minded and accountable for driving internal process changes that drive total cost reductions that will benefit all.

The correct pricing model supports the business and provides appropriate embedded incentives. It is important to understand implicitly that the outsource provider is a profit maximizer. This is reasonable, since few businesses are designed to be otherwise. Therefore, all parties should explore ways to encourage the outsource provider to optimize for the desired outcomes which will ultimately lead to additional profits for the service provider if performance objectives are met.

Is this a risky bet for a company and its service providers? Most thought leaders say no. But it is not easy. Adrian Gonzalez from ARC Advisory Group, a research and advisory firm that specializes in supply chain management and third-party logistics, offers this advice: "What differentiates Vested Outsourcing are not the risks, which are inherent in any outsourcing relationship, but the potential payoff for both service providers and customers. In other words, the benefits-to-risk ratio is much greater for Vested Outsourcing. And the risk of remaining at the status quo—in terms of lower profits for service providers and continued diminishing returns for customers—trumps them all."

It is especially difficult for organizations to build a dynamic relationship that challenges the status quo in existing processes. But properly structured Vested Outsourcing partnerships can—and do!—create paybacks for both parties.

Rule #5: Governance Structure Should Provide Insight, Not Merely Oversight

In the early days of outsourcing, many companies made the mistake of simply throwing the work over the fence to the outsource provider, with poorly defined requirements and often no performance metrics or service-level agreements. As scary as it may seem, we have seen some companies with a high percentage of outsource agreements operating under no formal governance structure. Fortunately, most companies that jumped into outsourcing have fixed this problem. The downside is that many have gone to the other extreme, as witnessed by companies experiencing ailment 9, measurement minutiae. Today's outsource providers often have a small army of program managers who micromanage the outsource provider.

An effective Vested Outsourcing partnership outsources to service providers that are real experts. Such partnerships should be managed to create a culture of insight, not oversight.

Let us look at the meaning of both words to get a better understanding of the difference.

> *Insight*: Power of acute observation and deduction; penetration, discernment, perception.
> *Oversight*: Watchful care; superintendence; general supervision.

If a company has done a good job picking the proper outsource provider, a trusted expert in its field, why does it need a small army providing general supervision? Our experience has shown that companies tend to go overboard and have a tendency to micromanage outsource providers. This is often due to ailment 4, the junkyard dog factor.

A properly designed governance structure should establish good insight, not provide layers of supervisory oversight.

HOW VESTED OUTSOURCING RULES WORK TOGETHER

In Vested Outsourcing, organizations work together on a foundation of trust where there is mutual accountability for achieving the desired outcomes.

Through the careful alignment of performance objectives, accountability, and control, the service provider, while absorbing additional risk, is empowered to pursue improvements that will deliver improved performance, higher profits, and lower total ownership cost.

Vested Outsourcing uses free market innovation to improve the outsourcing relationship. An innovative win-win Vested Outsourcing arrangement can be challenging to achieve, but the Vested Outsourcing journey should always strive to arrive at this idealized end state to achieve the three goals (performance pyramid where the companies consistently apply a WIIFWe foundation and all five of the Vested Outsourcing rules).

For service providers, Vested Outsourcing is an opportunity to exercise greater flexibility in deciding how support is provided, to ensure cash flow stability through long-term contracts, and to increase revenue by rewarding its investment in improving processes. For the company that is outsourcing, it is a chance to obtain improved performance while decreasing costs and assets by partnering with a highly competent and properly motivated firm.

Companies that want to embark on a Vested Outsourcing partnership should understand the central core of the WIIFWe approach and the Five Rules. They should treat them as rules to live by.

A Vested Outsourcing partnership that does not strictly adhere to the WIIFWe core and to the Five Rules can easily fall victim to one or more of the outsourcing ailments outlined in chapter 3.

SUCCESS STORIES (IT REALLY DOES WORK!)

The Wendy's ad from 1984 aptly asked: "Where's the beef?" That is, does this really work? Studying firms that have adopted a successful Vested Outsourcing philosophy with key suppliers is richly rewarding.

One downside is that they often view their work in Vested Outsourcing as a competitive advantage, so they want to protect their privacy. Companies do not want to promote the idea externally or allow their names to be used in a study, because this would aid their competitors and encourage customers to seek price reductions. In the study conducted by the University of Tennessee found that out of 20 participants, only 1 would allow its company name used in the written results.

Although the benefits of Vested Outsourcing partnerships have been espoused over the last ten years, the amount of coverage has been minimal.

One area that has published success stories is in the aerospace and aviation service sectors, especially in the area of outsourced logistics and maintenance support. The U.S Department of Defense (DoD) is probably one of the most active organizations promoting the application of Vested Outsourcing partnerships, known in the military sector as Performance-Based Logistics (PBL). PBL has more than 200 current and planned arrangements in place since it was first piloted in the DoD in1998. Documented case studies prove that performance-based agreements work at increasing performance while optimizing costs.[7]

One such program is the General Electric F404 Aircraft Engine program, which was the winner of a 2005 Secretary of Defense Award for Excellence for its work in helping revamp the Navy's spare parts planning and engine maintenance process for the F/A-18 Hornet, the Navy's frontline aircraft, which is powered by the GE F404 engine. There are 1,862 F404 engines installed in Hornet aircraft deployed around the globe. For two decades, all maintenance had been done within the Navy's internal depot structure.

In 2003, the Navy teamed with General Electric Aircraft Engines in a nine-and-a-half-year agreement. Under the agreement, GE brought its expertise in Lean manufacturing and Six Sigma process control to the joint Navy-GE team that was chartered to improve the maintenance process for the Hornet. The team researched, reinvented, and reengineered the repair and support functions for the F404 engine that led to dramatic results, including:

- Reducing repair turn time from 120 to 47 days
- Raising component availability from 50 to 92 percent, which in turn reduced the fleet total cost of ownership by $79 million
- Reducing fleet back orders by 100 percent, from 718 to 0
- Delivering 99 percent first-pass material availability
- Reducing depot work in process from 1,264 to 450 carcasses (engines off wing) by streamlining and reinventing processes

During the first two years of this agreement, GE exceeded all the agreed-on requirements. Not only has GE been able to increase the availability of the F/A-18 Hornet, one of the most important planes in the military arsenal, but it has been able to increase its profitability. This has been done by guaranteeing that parts are available when and where they are needed and that the engines spend time flying missions rather than waiting for maintenance and repairs.[8] GE has long been recognized as an innovator in product development, and their early adoption of Vested Outsourcing approaches to innovate in outsourced logistics and maintenance support have proved to be successful. Russ Sparks, GE's Vice President and General Manager of Military Systems states:

> The performance-based approach with the Navy F404 engine created a vested relationship between the Navy and GE that addressed Admiral Massenburg's real desire—to keep planes in the air. The contract was structured to align GE and Navy business metrics so both teams were pulling in the same direction. The business model and contract were no longer based on a 'consumption' model where GE made money by selling more spare parts. Instead, GE's profitability was tied closely to increased time-on-wing and availability metrics that were crucial to the Navy for keeping planes flying versus on the ground. The agreement encouraged GE's long-term investments and process innovation that drove improvements to the Navy's desired outcomes. GE, in turn, was rewarded with more profitability.

The DoD's results are not limited to simple incremental improvements in performance. It is not uncommon for its performance-based programs to report improvements of between 40 and 70 percent. Performance-based approaches have such a high potential that the Office of Management and Budget recently mandated that 45 percent of all services acquired by the DoD be procured through performance-based agreements.

TO GO THE WHOLE NINE YARDS OR NOT

It is important to keep in mind that just because a company *can* do Vested Outsourcing for just about anything it might outsource, this

Figure 4.4   Vested Outsourcing Decision Matrix

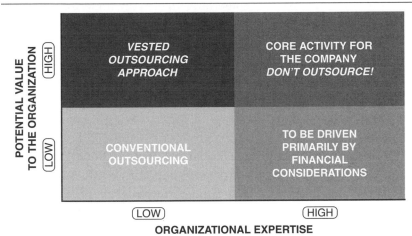

does not mean that it should. Some activities still should be outsourced conventionally. For example, office supply purchases are not strategically critical for most firms. Vested Outsourcing is hard and takes time; it should be done only in the areas that will have the largest impact or return for the company.

Companies can evaluate their outsourcing opportunities using the chart in Figure 4.4. If there is high value and expertise to continue to manage a process within the company, do not outsource those activities. However, if there is low expertise but high value, that activity is a good target for Vested Outsourcing. Conventional outsourcing is best used when contracts do not add strategic value to operations. Look for opportunities to decrease cost, increase availability, and thus increase customer satisfaction.

If Vested Outsourcing looks promising for an activity, ask yourself not "What's in it for me?" but rather "What's in it for *we*?" to be successful.

WHAT'S IN IT FOR WE? IDENTIFYING THE PONY

Before deciding to undertake a Vested Outsourcing agreement, validate the opportunity. A critical component of successful Vested Outsourcing, and one of the first steps, is to conduct a baseline assessment and to identify what we refer to as "the Pony." We call it the Pony because it represents the pure happiness that one would see on children's faces when they learn they can get a Pony for Christmas. After all, what young child does not want a Pony? It is something that many hope for and most never get.

It also represents what Ronald Reagan used to portray as the optimist approach. Reagan used to tell a story about a man who came upon a young boy excitedly digging through a large pile of manure. "What are you doing, son?" the man asked. "Well, sir," the boy answered happily, "with all of this manure, there must be a Pony in here somewhere!"[9]

In Vested Outsourcing, the Pony is the difference between the value of the current solution and the potential optimized solution. It represents something the outsourcing company wants but was not able to get on its own or with existing service providers. Or, to cite James Collins and Jerry Porras from their popular *Harvard Business Review* article, it is a BHAG, a Big Hairy Audacious Goal.[10] Remember the $400,000 that could be saved annually by redesigning the package? That $400,000 is the Pony.

In order to determine the size of the Pony, let alone its existence, you must establish a baseline. Baselining is key because it identifies the Pony's value, which helps determine the combination of service-level improvements and cost-savings potential. The service provider and company outsourcing should use this concept to help derive the appropriate incentive levels provided to the service provider. The bigger the potential prize, the bigger the incentives the service provider should have the chance to earn.

If the outsource provider can find the Pony by achieving service-level and cost targets, everyone will be happy because the outsourcing company finally gets what it wants. The catch: The company has to share the value of the Pony with the outsource provider that helped achieve it. This value is used to fund the incentives for the outsource provider.

GETTING STARTED

How do you get started transforming the outsourcing effort? Can your outsourcing agreement go the whole nine yards? Start by reviewing the ten common ailments outlined in chapter 3 to see which ones apply. Then ask how the company got there. Once you fully understand the problem, explore the Five Rules of Vested Outsourcing and how they can help. Some of the key questions to begin asking are:

- What are the desired outcome (not what activities will you outsource)?
- Who will be impacted?
- Is there a Pony?
- What is the outsourcing business model that will best capture the Pony?
- How can the contract be structured to support the business model in order to prevent perverse incentives?

If you cannot answer those questions clearly and confidently, do not proceed further before you can do so. Everything depends on clear answers to the questions.

When the decision is made to explore Vested Outsourcing, use a structured framework to help you transform your existing outsourcing relationship to a more productive performance-based approach.

That framework is explored in detail in chapters 6 to 10.

CHAPTER 5

THE GAME-CHANGING ECONOMICS OF VESTED OUTSOURCING

It is much easier to say win-win than to execute win-win.

People play to win. From grade school on we are conditioned to believe that there is a winner and a loser. To have two winners on different teams must require some new math or letting somcone win. For the truly competitive, giving in or sharing does not come easily. After all, there is only so much pie to go around.

When this attitude is mixed with perverse incentives, dramatic negative results can occur.

Yet, deep down, if we really think about it, we realize that the amount of pie is not a fixed amount. More pie is made by sharing and creating conditions where everyone can win. However, a strong trusting relationship is required to achieve mutual success.

Perhaps a classic example of this type of relationship is a healthy marriage. More "pie," or benefits, are derived by the couple working together than they can achieve by working alone. Based on the next statistics, it is clear that married men fare much better than their single counterparts.

- The Office of National Statistics found that single men age 45 and over are at a 23 percent greater risk of early death.[1]
- Married men earn more money than their single counterparts.
- Insurance rates are higher for single men than married men.

If the amount of pie were fixed, the benefits gained by the husband somehow would come at the expense of the wife. Yet married women also fair better in marriage than not.

- Single women have mortality rates that are 50 percent higher than married women.
- Having a spouse can decrease your risk for dying from cancer as much as adding ten years to your life. Single people spend longer in the hospital, and have a greater risk of dying after surgery.[2]
- Married women are 30 percent more likely to rate their health as excellent or very good compared to single women and 40 percent less likely to rate their health as only fair or poor compared to single women.[3]

How does marriage and mortality apply to economics and outsourcing? Simply this: Economics can and does validate the benefits of developing a win-win relationship. This chapter explores two economic principles behind Vested Outsourcing: behavioral economics and the economics of innovation. Applying these two principles to your outsourcing agreement will improve the efficiencies and the effectiveness of the outsourcing relationship that creates the win-win model.

PRINCIPLE 1: BEHAVIORAL ECONOMICS

Behavioral economics—or the study of incentives and strategic interactions—has been researched since the 1940s, when John von Neumann and Oskar Morgenstern applied mathematical analysis to modeling competition and cooperation in living things. Its application has ranged from studying simple organisms to the complex interactions of human beings. Behavioral economics is more popularly referred to as game theory because it attempts to model human behaviors, especially when there is an incentive at stake. Specifically, game theory attempts to model how an individual's success in making a strategic decision depends on the choices of others.

According to economists, two types of games can be played: zero-sum games and non–zero-sum games. In the case of zero-sum games, the size of the pie is fixed. For one participant to get more, other participants must get less. In non–zero-sum games, the size of the pie is not fixed; therefore, everyone can do better or much worse.

Deeply rooted in mathematics, game theory began to raise eyebrows when John Nash, a Princeton University mathematician and game theorist, published his theory of equilibrium in 1950, commonly called the Nash equilibrium. For this contribution, Nash received the 1994 Nobel Prize in economics, shared with John C. Harsanyi and Reinhard Selten.[4]

One of the core principles of game theory that Nash made famous—and the one that is of particular interest to Vested Outsourcing—is the concept of equilibrium. Equilibrium is also referred to a *solution concept*. One of the key philosophies of game theory is to develop the strategy that will optimize for the payoff (results). Nash's early work in game theory led to what is commonly known as the Nash equilibrium. In a game involving two or more players, the Nash equilibrium occurs when each player has chosen a strategy and no player can benefit by changing his or her strategy while the other players keep their strategy unchanged. For instance, Unilever and Wal-Mart would be in Nash equilibrium if Unilever makes the best decision possible, taking into account Wal-Mart's decision, and Wal-Mart makes the best decision possible, taking into account Unilever's decision.

According to the Nash equilibrium, you should devise your strategy *relative to the other player's strategy*. In short, a player's optimized payoff can and often is constrained based on a competing player's strategy and assumes the other player is playing against you. But can you do better? Can you improve your payoff? Later economists have studied game theory further and shown that it is possible to improve results beyond that of a Nash equilibrium. *The key lies in players working together toward a mutually beneficial strategy that optimizes for the cumulative payoff.* In other words, the power of partnerships and collaboration is not to optimize for the status quo (e.g., Nash equilibrium) but to look for ways to change the game to create an overall larger payoff. In short, the size of the pie is not fixed, and companies can and should work together to find ways to make more pie.

At the heart of game theory is the statistical rigor that illustrates what can happen when people play to win. Rational individuals will default to decisions that optimize for their best position. In simple terms, people's natural tendency is to play to win, especially if they believe that the size of the pie is fixed (a zero-sum game). Game theory models situations and game rules and how people react to the rules in their effort to win the game. By studying the rules of games and the reactions of players, game theorists have mathematically proven that seemingly innocuous rules can cause participants to do things to optimize their outcome, such as income, even when doing so might not make the most strategic sense.[5]

Cooperative (Win-Win) Games

Modern game theorists have taken the concepts of game theory to new levels by applying them to cooperative, or win-win, games. A win-win game is one that is designed in a way where all participants can benefit. In economics, this is called a non–zero-sum game.

How might we apply these lessons to an outsourcing situation? One of the most common outsourcing problems is when companies fall into the conventional trap of beating up their suppliers on price. They wrongly assume that they are operating in a zero-sum game and that the only way to cut costs is to get it from the supplier. The total gains and losses will sum to zero. One side wins, one side loses.

A zero-sum game attitude is typical in conventional outsourcing negotiations and is a key reason why many of today's outsourcing relationships fail to deliver the benefits that could be realized to all parties. Chapter 1 revealed the dynamics of everyone giving their all for their particular role. A zero-sum game attitude is what drove Stream International sales reps and business managers to react the way they did. Each was optimizing for his or her position.

Robert Axelrod's book *The Evolution of Cooperation* helped put the concept of win-win game theory on the map. The book describes computer games with participants from around the world, focusing on determining how individuals in groups that are likely to interact with others act in a competitive situation. These computer game simulations statistically prove that when individuals cooperate, they come out better than when they do not.[6]

The lessons are simple yet profound. Playing a game together to achieve a mutual interest is always better than playing it with self-interest in mind. Ergo the philosophy that working together toward a win-win strategy is always better than a win-lose strategy aimed at promoting self-interest.[7]

Let us use an example of one easy-to-understand computer game that proves the concept. In the game, there are two players, and each plays 20 rounds of a game where they choose to "cooperate" or "command." Each decision has a specific payoff. If the game was played with the goal of maximizing winnings, the winner would be the player who earns the most winnings possible. When the winnings are looked at on an individual basis, when one player commands and the other cooperates, the commanding party earns $3 and the cooperator earns nothing. If both choose to cooperate, each earns $2. If both opt to command, each earns $1 (see Figure 5.1).

In the game, each player decides if they want to "cooperate" or "command" and presses a button that corresponds with their decision. The total payoff for a 20-round game in which one player always commands and the other always cooperates is $60, with one player winning everything and the other nothing. This is a very rare result. At the other extreme, where both players always command or play to maximize their individual reward, the total game payoff is $40, or $20 per player. However, the most profitable strategy is when both players approach the game with a mind-set of mutual cooperation from start to finish. In this case, the total game payoff is the highest: $80. Those truly wanting to optimize the solution for the biggest payoff should strategically agree on a cooperative strategy from the outset, as illustrated in Figure 5.2. The challenge then becomes not how to play to win against the other player but how to determine how to divide the extra payoff.

The moral is that players take a risk each time they become greedy for a little bit more because it makes the entire cooperative strategy

Figure 5.1   Payoff Matrix

	Player 2 Cooperate	Player 2 Command
Player 1 Cooperate	Player 1 = 2 Player 2 = 2 **Payoff = 4**	Player 1 = 0 Player 2 = 3 **Payoff = 3**
Player 1 Command	Player 1 = 3 Player 2 = 0 **Payoff = 3**	Player 1 =1 Player 2 = 1 **Payoff = 2**

Figure 5.2   Win-Lose Matrix

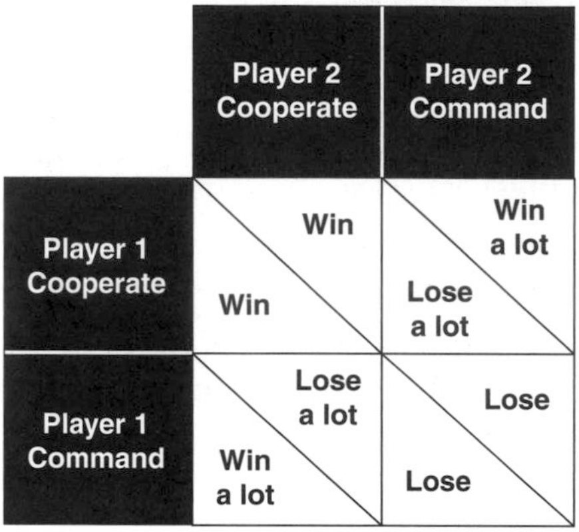

fall apart, and both emerge poorer.[8] In game theory terminology, when both players cooperate, the payoff is a win-win; when one player cooperates and the other player commands, the payoff is a win-lose; and when both players command, the payoff is a lose-lose.

This example of the game reinforces the idea of the Pony, a concept introduced in chapter 4. In this case, the maximum game payoff of complete command strategy, or when both parties approach the game to win at the expense of the other party, is $40. If they cooperate from the start, the maximum game payoff is $80. The difference of $40 is the Pony. In mathematical terms, the Pony is the difference between the value of the *self-optimized solution* and the potential of an *optimized collaborative solution*, or the potential return in the relationship.

Mike Shor, an associate professor at the Owen Graduate School of Management of Vanderbilt University in Nashville, Tennessee, is a leader in bringing game theory to the business world. He comments: "Sometimes game theory is mistakenly viewed as the study of conflict, particularly with the literature on zero-sum games in which I win and you lose. But, in business, one of the most important contributions of game theory is to help us understand how both parties can win. That's a very fundamental contribution that game theory has to make to business."[9]

How can a company apply game theory to outsourcing? Leading companies are starting to realize what economists have proven; they need to work together to win together. Cooperation should be a key component of a business's outsourcing strategy. Unfortunately, business executives have been hard-wired for most of the twentieth century to play business like sports with a clear winner and loser. Today's thought-leading business strategists are starting to promote the concept that sports are simply a bad analogy for business.[10]

Bottom line: Behavioral economics is real, and it is powerful. Eight Nobel prizes have been awarded to game theorists. Based on the idea that contracts are zero-sum games, we have created flawed structures, suboptimal contractual agreements, and wary relationships. Once the problem is recognized, smart business leaders will begin to think strategically about designing a win-win outsourcing solution with their most strategic suppliers so that both parties can optimize for a better overall solution.

Importance of Rules

Winning starts with understanding the rules. These rules of the game, whether they are laws, business norms, or corporate policies, can impact the outcome.[11] Card games and sports are regulated by clear sets of rules that define the games themselves. Take baseball. There is no point in a batter arguing that he or she should be allowed to swing and miss 15 times. The rule is three strikes and you are out. Period. In business, rules are not so clear-cut.

In the world of outsourcing, there is no clearly defined set of rules. In a conventional outsourcing arrangement, businesses come together and strike a deal where the service provider gets paid for performing transactions. Outside of a statement of work and the pricing, there are no rules to define the practice of outsourcing. For this reason, companies go into an outsource relationship to win because that is the same strategy they use with their customers. If there is no alternative, the current solution fills the void. As we have discussed, optimizing for our own self-interest will most likely be doomed to a win-lose strategy that ultimately will hurt the return on an outsourcing project.

To take the example one step further, in card games and sports games, the rules are fixed and communicated in advance. If you want to play, you have to abide by the rules. Running directly to third base without going to first or second based may indeed be shorter, but such shortcuts only add confusion on the field of play. In outsourcing, the rules are typically not known or fixed.

Unfortunately, organizations do not publish the outsourcing rules they play by, and are always looking for shortcuts. Changing the rules is not only tolerated—it is often expected.

Recently a Fortune 50 company reported less than stellar margins due in part to the declining economy. The company has a vast supplier and outsourcing network and spends billions of dollars in outsourcing. As soon as quarterly earnings hit Wall Street, the company brought the hammer down on its suppliers to reduce prices by 20 percent. It did not matter that contracts were in place; the company changed the rules to suit its needs. Suppliers either played under the new rules or lost business.

Rarely do companies establish and keep track of the rules of the outsourcing game. Companies have jumped into outsourcing without understanding core principles of creating a solid relationship and business model. The Five Rules are so powerful because they give everyone an equal basis on which to develop and strengthen their outsourcing relationship.

Changing the Rules of the Game

One fundamental of business strategy is that you should actively shape the game you play, not just play the game you find. Do not accept the rules of the game as they stand; shape them so that everyone can win. This contemporary thinking is outlined in a book by Adam Brandenburger and Barry Nalebuff, *Co-opetition*.[12]

Let us go back to the analogy of sharing a pie and how changing the rules can benefit the parties. Conventional thinking is that the fairest approach is simply to share the pie—with each party getting a slice of the exact same size. Behavioral economics, however, has shown that our natural tendency is to want to optimize and win, which means getting the bigger piece of the pie. Under conventional thinking, when one party wins and gets a larger piece of the pie, it comes at the expense of the other party who is playing (this is a zero-sum game), who gets a smaller piece. But what if we could increase the size of the pie? In other words, instead of trying to divide up the current pie, what if we look for more pies? Then we are no longer locked into looking at the pie we have but at all the pies that are out there.

Under this new scenario, all parties in the game (an outsourcing relationship) are motivated to work together to increase the overall size of the pie, with each receiving a bigger piece by working together. In this case, it is a non-zero-sum game, as the size of the pie increases without a negative impact on others in the game. Establishing predefined rules with positive outcomes for the players ensures that all parties bring their best thinking to see how they can make the biggest possible pie (e.g., increase revenue, decrease waste, cut cycle time).

Let us go back to the Nash equilibrium, where each player has chosen a strategy and no player can benefit by changing his or her strategy while the other players keep their strategy unchanged. We have seen that many outsourcing agreements fail because the parties have reached Nash equilibrium, are unwilling to change their strategy, and view the pie as a fixed amount. Vested Outsourcing, based on win-win game theory, emphasizes the importance of cooperation, sharing, and overall group success in contrast to domination and personal gain. All players are treated as equally important and valuable, and all work to find the strategy that grows the size of the pie. *Vested Outsourcing is the strategic game changer* because it provides the framework to change the point of equilibrium in the outsourcing relationship into a real win-win strategy.

PRINCIPLE 2: ECONOMICS OF INNOVATION

Although it is easy to agree that everyone should work together in a win-win environment, many junkyard dogs question if an outsource provider really can grow the pie at all. Certainly not every agreement has a Pony; that is why—in chapter 7—we discuss the steps needed to validate the legitimacy of a Pony or, in other words, of growing the pie. Absent the existence of a significant upside for all parties, there is no need to develop a Vested Outsourcing strategy with the supplier. Vested Outsourcing is not practical or rewarding in zero-sum games and uses a non-zero-sum game as one of its basic assumptions.

Our experience has shown us that the majority of outsourced programs do indeed have a significant opportunity to improve. The question then is how we can make the pie bigger. What can be done to grow it rapidly, so that all parties benefit? An understanding of the importance of innovation is key to making this connection.

Importance of Innovation

Given today's dynamic environment, businesses must use innovation to change the game.[13] Two primary misconceptions are associated with innovation. The first is the confusion between invention and innovation. The second is that innovation applies only to research and development (R&D) of new products or services.

Let's start with the first misconception—confusing invention and innovation. For our purposes, invention has at its heart the idea that something—an idea, a concept, a physical element—is created or constructed that did not exist before. The telephone is an example of an invention. Innovation, however, is modifying what already exists. It is continuous and incremental in nature. Cynthia Barton Rabe, author of *The Innovation Killer,* defines innovation as "the application of an idea that results in a valuable improvement."[14] Telephone innovations led to cordless devices and the development of cell phones.

It is dangerous to rely solely on inventions for future revenue streams. Doing so ignores the significant revenue streams that can come through continual improvements of a product or service. Innovations can be risky, but doing nothing is more so. As the economist Joseph Schumpeter put it, companies that resist change are "standing on ground that is crumbling beneath their feet."[15]

The second myth is that innovation applies only to R&D in terms of developing new products and services. The American Productivity and Quality Center (APQC) is an advocate in debunking this myth. The center's studies have shown that innovation applies in virtually all parts of a company and its underlying processes. One area where innovation has been mostly untapped is in business operations. The vast majority of companies that rushed to outsource focused on shifting activities to suppliers rather than making the business more effective through business model innovation.

However, a few organizations are using outsourcing as a springboard to create entirely new ways of doing business and new tools to support breakthrough efficiency gains. IBM chief executive officer (CEO) Samuel J. Palmisano is stressing innovation in how IBM works: "The way you will thrive in this environment is by innovating—innovating in technologies, innovating in strategies, innovating in business models."[16]

Although companies can and do innovate internally, some of the world's best are realizing that they need to work outside of their companies to drive innovation at a much greater rate. One of the earliest adopters of this philosophy was Bill Joy, the founder of Sun Microsystems. Joy's Law clearly illustrates this thinking: "No matter who you are, most of the bright people don't work for you."[17] In today's complex business environment, companies must strategically turn to their outsourcing suppliers in order to gain access to creativity and skills through a global network of specialized workers and engineers.[18]

Progressive companies are applying Joy's Law by turning to outsource providers not merely to perform an activity but rather as creative minds with expert talent in their field of specialty. For these companies, outsourcing is not simply about transferring activities; it is about working with the best of the best providers to drive innovative business practices across virtually all major corporate functions. Microsoft is an example of an innovative company that is turning to outsource providers to help it speed innovation.

"We use partners to gain access to capabilities we don't possess. They have a huge impact on our ability to innovate that goes way beyond low cost and allows us to achieve significant advantages in time to market, results that we could not realize working with just our own resources," says Mak Agashe, general manager for Windows Serviceability at Microsoft.[19]

Companies are entering into longer-term, collaborative environments based on the Vested Outsourcing rules, rules that are designed to reward innovation, to solve real business problems, and to create exponential productivity gains. Another progressive company that is applying Joy's Law is Procter & Gamble (P&G). A. G. Lafley, former CEO of P&G, developed an approach called "Connect and Develop." Its core principle was to invite innovation from outside of the company. What this approach did was build an incredibly busy innovation network that welcomed commercial opportunities whenever and wherever they presented themselves.[20] Under the strategy, P&G seeks external partners that have already made investments in equipment, processes, and tools. Doing this allows P&G to leverage its infostructure instead of adding costly infrastructure.[21]

P&G's "Connect and Develop" model increased R&D productivity by more than 50 percent and doubled the success rate of new products. The organization went from innovating with barely 20 percent involvement from external resources to 35 percent by 2006.[22] But can this innovation apply in areas outside of product R&D? The answer is yes. P&G

has since reached levels of 50 percent of its technology, product, and service innovation through external sources. The principles of the new model unleashed a new set of opportunities, many of which yielded substantial benefits.[23]

In short, leading organizations recognize that innovation can be enhanced, stimulated, or improved by using external resources in their outsourcing relationships. The pie just got bigger.

Although business leaders agree that innovation can yield great benefits, almost all will also point to the fact that investing in innovation involves costs and risks that could have a negative effect if the efforts do not result in successful end products or services. For this reason, it is very important to provide the right economic incentives to motivate win-win behavior with outsource providers.

If outsource providers perceive all risk and no reward, they are most likely to take the conservative approach and not invest their own money on behalf of their customer, especially if they think benefits will not be shared. Going back to the pie analogy, what makes the players want to play the game? Why should suppliers invest their own money and put their best and brightest talent on developing a larger overall pie if their customers will not give them a larger piece? This is where the concept of the Pony comes into play.

Finding the Pony funds the *reward,* and the reward needs to be shared according to preestablished rules of the game based on risk allocation. The higher the risk taken, the higher the reward received. The concept of rewarding for innovative ideas is one deeply rooted in Adam Smith's philosophies of capitalism. Smith's basic proposition of economic theory is that an individual will invest in a resource—for example, land, equipment, or labor—most likely to earn the highest possible return for a given level of risk. Otherwise, the individual will use the resource where a higher rate of return can be gained. This philosophy is the foundation of mainstream economic theory.

Let us consider the example of risk and reward as it relates to innovation. Before protection in the form of patent law, there was little incentive to innovate, and thus inventions were uncommon. Recognition of this problem came in the form of the first patent law, enacted in Venice in 1474. It stated:

We have among us men of great genius, apt to invent and discover ingenious devices; and in view of the grandeur and virtue of our city more such men come to us every day from diverse parts. Now if provision were made for the works and devices discovered by such persons, so that others who see them could not build them and take the inventor's honor away, more men would then apply their genius, would discover, and would build devices of great utility and benefit to our commonwealth.[24]

Let us fast forward to the mid-1700s and look at James Watt—the inventor of the steam engine—as a classic example of the need for reward as motivator for innovation. In 1758 Watt began to repair apparatuses and equipment at the University of Glasgow. In 1763, he got the opportunity to work on his first Newcomen steam engine. His creative mind and hands tinkered with that model, and he produced a much-improved working model in 1765.

Watt lacked the needed capital to create a full-scale engine. He joined forces with John Roebuck, founder of the celebrated Carron Iron Works. Roebuck invested in Watt's ideas in the hope of a greater return on his investment. Without capital, Watt's steam engine project would have surely died. Much capital was spent in pursuing the groundbreaking Patent No. 913 in 1769. Watt labored on creating working prototypes but became strapped for resources when Roebuck went bankrupt. Watt was forced to take up employment as a surveyor until he managed to get an extension to his patent in 1775.

Matthew Boulton, a wealthy manufacturer who owned the Soho foundry works near Birmingham, England, acquired the patent rights and retained Watt to resume his work on the steam engine. The patent extension and the promise of a breakthrough device that would revolutionize productivity again entered the picture. Watt and Boulton formed a hugely successful partnership that lasted for the next 25 years and resulted in the modern-day steam engine. Boulton's investment of capital and Watt's investment of time paid off handsomely.

The lesson is simple. Innovation would not have been possible without the promise of a potential reward.

Intellectual property gurus Mark Blaxill and Ralph Eckardt sum it up best in their book *The Invisible Edge, Taking Your Strategy to the Next Level Using Intellectual Property*: "There's a reason that America has become the world's most innovative economy. It's because invention is an economic activity and patent rights encourage inventors to invest.

Without a reward system inventors' economics suffer and their incentive disappears."[25]

Ensuring protection for innovation is so steeped in American culture that President Lincoln endorsed patent laws in a speech that said economic incentives for innovation "added the *fuel of interest to the fire of genius* [emphasis added], in the discovery and production of new and useful things."[26] Innovation has built the world into what it is today; but innovation would not get funded without the hope of reward. Economist Paul Romer put it this way: "Technological change is the result of intentional actions taken by people who respond to market incentives."[27] Inventors such as Thomas Edison, the Wright brothers, Alexander Graham Bell, and many others have achieved great wealth from their innovations.

Significance of Brains versus Brawn

Common sense tells us that innovation helps drive improvements in the marketplace. But just how important is innovation? Conventional wisdom among business leaders and economics was that economic growth came primarily from labor and physical capital, such as investment in plant and machinery. In the 1950s, economist Robert Solow was one of the first to try to better understand the impact of innovation. Solow studied what he termed *technical change*, meaning improvements in business process or technical improvements in products, driven by innovation. His works concluded that less than 13 percent of economic growth could be explained by labor and physical capital; the remaining 87 percent came from technical change, or the brainpower to create innovative solutions.[28]

Jacob Schmookler and Moses Abramovitz came to the same conclusion as Solow in separate research. They all agreed that the element they called technical change accounted for 80 to 90 percent of total per capita income growth. By the 1980s, economists commonly believed that the economy was increasingly reliant on brains rather than brawn.[29] More recent research by the intellectual property pioneers Blaxill and Eckardt shows that companies that innovate rapidly profit the most.[30]

The most progressive innovators are now turning to their outsource providers as a source of innovation, especially in the area of operational efficiency and effectiveness. One of these pioneering innovators is Intel. Intel has long known that innovation pays. Innovation is what keeps

Moore's Law going. It is the competitive need to find better solutions sooner than others. Gordon Moore, cofounder of Intel Corp., observed that the number of transistors per square inch on a microprocessor chip had doubled each year since the integrated circuit had been invented, which led to his well-known prediction that the number of transistors on a chip would double every 18 months. (He later changed this figure to every two years.[31]) Engineers inside and outside of Intel keep the company running fast with new solutions and rapid progress in order to realize Moore's Law. Their incentive? If they follow Moore's Law they are able to keep ahead of the market and reap the financial rewards with premium pricing.[32] This emphasis on innovation is one of the primary reasons for Intel's interest in Vested Outsourcing.

With all the focus on innovation, we find it hard to believe that so many businesspeople are not applying the core concept of developing trusted outsourcing partnerships based more on brains than brawn. Companies continue to suffer from the outsourcing paradox by simply shifting work to the outsource provider and drawing a box around the scope of work to contain thinking to inside the service provider's four walls. Smart companies, however, are applying Joy's Law and are beginning to turn to the real power of outsourcing, which is to tap into the incredible potential brainpower of outsource providers that have made excelling at certain skills their core competency. Unfortunately, too many companies have built transaction-based outsourcing agreements that reward for brawn: paying for extraneous personnel, touches in manufacturing, hands in picking and packing, and fingers in data entry. Progressive companies are starting to apply what economists have proven: brains are better than brawn.

Integrating Rewards into Your Outsourcing Agreements

From a service provider perspective, the only reason to invest in innovation for the client is if there is a clear beneficial outcome: the Pony. As discussed in chapter 2, much of the work outsourced today has evolved to commodity status with respect to the activities performed within the four walls of a service provider.

Without the expectation of increased revenue or profit or other benefit, an outsource provider has little incentive to invest in innovation. Although service providers can and usually do invest in processes that benefit all customers, often they frown on client-specific innovation as risky business. This is especially true when companies that outsource regularly shop the marketplace on price. Making an investment is often a long-term decision. If the outsource providers invest, and thus raise their costs, before they receive the promise of a payoff, they are likely to come in on the short end of a competitive bid based solely on price.

But without innovation, the opportunity for growth is minimal for both organizations, and returns and shareholder value suffer for the companies. To solve this problem, outsourcing agreements should integrate rewards that encourage investments that benefit client-specific needs or that create a competitive advantage for the company outsourcing.

Speaking to the heart of Vested Outsourcing, organizations that want to strengthen their market and financial position should form partnerships that share commitments, risks, and rewards (Rule #4). Leading organizations are turning to carefully crafted arrangements that go well beyond service-level agreements that share risk and gains. Our research found four outstanding studies relating to this concept in addition to our work at the University of Tennessee, as listed in Figure 5.3:

Figure 5.3   Suggested Additional Reading

Source	Summary
Peter Holmes **Creating the Link Between Innovation and Outsourcing—Opportunities for the UK Public Sector to Take the Lead** *Source:* http://www.accenture.com/Global/Research_and_Insights/By_Industry/Government_and_Public_Service/CreatingLead.htm web accessed April 18, 2009	Executives around the world who believe they have used outsourcing to achieve dramatic results attribute the results largely to structuring their outsourcing arrangements to share risks and gains with their business partners
APQC and IBM **Successfully Embedding Innovation: Strategies and Tactics** Source: APQC Publications, 2007	Best-practice partners in this study not only embedded innovation into their mission statements, they established rewards and performance systems and applied the approach to the way they engaged with their customers and business partners. Rewards and recognition for innovating are publicized in these successful organizations so that they act as positive reinforcements and incentives for future efforts.[1]

(Continued)

Figure 5.3   Continued

Source	Summary
Mark Blaxill and Ralph Eckardt *The Invisible Edge, Taking Your Strategy to the Next Level Using Intellectual Property* Source: Penguin Group (USA) Inc., New York 2009	Case studies on P&G, Eli Lilly, and Toyota
MacCormack, Forbath, Brooks, and Kalaher *Innovation through Global Collaboration: A New Source of Competitive Advantage* Source: Harvard Business School, HBS Working Paper 07–079, August 2007	The HBS study revealed that leading firms include contract terms that govern the payment of rewards, which aim to align the incentives of client and partner. These firms went further than common service level agreement terms in sharing risks with partners and rewarding them for their *"top-line"* impact. Partners willingly absorbed costs knowing that payments would be tied to revenues or profits. In some cases, the arrangements went as far as providing stakes in the business to partners.[2]

[1] APQC and IBM, "Successfully Embedding Innovation: Strategies and Tactics," *APQC Publications* (2007).
[2] MacCormack, Forbath, Brooks, and Kalaher, op cit.

Perhaps the most noteworthy example of taking open innovation to the next level is provided by Toyota Motor Company, one of the most bench-marked organizations in the world. In an industry where supplier price, quality, and innovation are critical to product value, Toyota is arguably the best at recognizing the need to engage suppliers in healthy competition balanced with risk and gain sharing.

Traditionally the relationship between carmakers and their suppliers can only be described as contentious. As we showed in the explanation of game theory, issues arise in the relationships because cost-cutting initiatives take precedence over cooperation—usually ending up hurting the suppliers as carmakers try to drive prices down. Of course, for auto-makers leveraging purchases in excess of $100 billion, pennies saved in supplier pricing can have a considerable impact on the bottom line. These purchasing tactics, though, are a classic zero-sum game: shifting profits away from the suppliers to the carmaker's bottom line.[33]

Toyota, however, recognized that the importance of supplier technology and innovation overrides the tendency to shift to zero-sum game practices. It understood that suppliers need to make money also, and created an environment that encouraged suppliers to invest in improving their designs and processes leading to lower cost structures and higher margins for the suppliers. Thus, Toyota structured a collaborative model that shared ownership interests in a network of suppliers and outsourced assemblers. Known as keiretsu, the model involved Toyota taking an ownership position in its suppliers' businesses and vice versa for some key suppliers. The incentive for these Toyota Group members was the direct alignment of financial and technical improvement interests with Toyota.[34]

Embedded in the norms of Toyota's collaboration network is the equitable reward system and the key principle that there is an obligation to *share* ideas. As a result, improvements in the entire network contribute 10 percent to Toyota's net income. And it results in win-win innovation: Toyota's supplier community has improved its quality and productivity performance in innovative alignment with the improvements in Toyota itself. The result is increased competitive advantage all around. Continuous improvement through sharing risk and reward in the Toyota network has made not just the components themselves but the final stage of assembly more competitive as well. Toyota figured out how to help its suppliers improve their game at nearly the same scale as Toyota itself—a benchmark for incentives.[35]

The Toyota supplier network provides a good example of organizing for collaborative and innovative success. Governance for sharing the benefits in both financial and competitive gain through the rules associated with network intellectual property (IP) set the stage for strong commercial trust and confidence that the whole network will share in the benefits of high performance.[36]

In the Toyota Group, the rules of the game and the reward structure are clearly laid out. Terms of membership include ownership equity and clear guidelines for members to actively engage in the collaborative community linked by shared development work, shared improvement initiatives, and shared property. Toyota and its suppliers—really component competitors—are organized to share knowledge; thus, they overlook short-term gain for the long-term network gain. Operational knowledge, including cost, quality, inventory management, and the like, is considered the property of the network, accessible to all, although some confidentiality among direct competitors is recognized. The clearly understood rule that Toyota states is: "*The price of entry into the network is a limited ability to protect proprietary production knowledge. Intellectual property rights reside at the network, rather than firm, level* [emphasis in original]."

Thus, incentives for innovation with partners need not always be totally financial. They can simply be the avoidance of the negative impact in market share, growth, and profit as a result of competitors implementing a more successful approach to innovation. An open and flexible approach to IP management can allow partners to access the outsourcing organization's noncompetitive IP or share newly developed IP, as long as the uses are not competitive.[37] In addition, longer contract terms can be part of an innovation incentive package.

GETTING STARTED

We have seen in this chapter that science supports two key premises of Vested Outsourcing: developing "win-win" outsourcing agreements and rewarding appropriately for risks taken and for innovation. We have learned from game theory and innovation economics that a balanced relationship between partners is crucial.

We began this chapter by professing that it is much easier to say win-win than to execute it. That is why a large part of the University of Tennessee's efforts focused on developing a comprehensive implementation approach to help guide companies through all the steps needed to transform a conventional outsourcing relationship to a Vested Outsourcing one.

Chapters 6 to 10 explore the implementation framework and share insights on how best to proceed.

PART III

VESTING
THE PARTNERSHIP

CHAPTER 6

LAY THE FOUNDATION

A Vested Outsourcing journey begins well before the initiation of the contract and transcends the contract itself.

In conventional outsourcing, the tendency is to think that once the contract is signed, the job is completed. But this is essentially like giving birth to a baby and thinking that the job is done. The parents among us are well aware that, as painful as delivery may be, in many ways it is the easy part, as it has a defined beginning and end. The next 18 to 21 years are when the character of the relationship is defined, refined, and deepened. Think of Vested Outsourcing as a lifelong relationship, not as a short-term project.

FRAMEWORK FOR IMPLEMENTATION

Many of the problems with conventional outsourcing arrangements stem from jumping straight to contract negotiations without a solid understanding of the ramifications. For this reason, we recommend a five-phase approach, as illustrated Figure 6.1. Note that establishing the contract does not occur until the fourth phase.

All of the steps are crucial to the successful implementation of Vested Outsourcing, but there is no one-size-fits-all approach. The steps do not have to be performed sequentially; each team may determine which order to perform them in and the level of effort necessary to achieve each step. Some steps may be reordered to fit your needs. However, our research and experience shows that all of these steps must be taken at some point in order to achieve a successful

Figure 6.1   Vested Outsourcing Implementation Plan

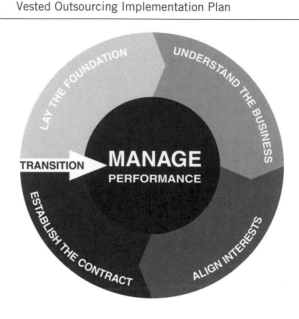

Vested Outsourcing business model. Skipping steps usually results in a poorly conceived business model agreement, lengthening the time needed to implement a Vested Outsourcing program, or a total disconnect in what the service provider is doing versus what the customer actually wanted.

We examine the five subprocesses of the Vested Outsourcing Implementation framework:

1.   Lay the foundation.
2.   Understand the business.
3.   Align interests.
4.   Establish the contract.
5.   Manage performance.

As mentioned in chapter 4, just because you *can* do Vested Outsourcing for just about anything does not mean you *should*. Some things still should be conventionally outsourced. Vested Outsourcing is hard and it takes time; it should really be done only for the areas that will have a large payoff or impact on the firm. Use the Evaluation

Matrix introduced in chapter 4 (Figure 4.4) to determine those opportunities that can or should not be outsourced. Do not outsource core processes that are of high value to the company; they are critical to the firm. Excellent targets for Vested Outsourcing are areas where there is low internal expertise (perhaps managing a warehouse, facility management) and those opportunities where you can save significant resources (personnel, financial). Use conventional outsourcing when contracts do not add strategic value to operations. In these cases, look for significant opportunities to decrease cost, increase availability, and thus increase customer satisfaction.

UNDERSTAND THE OPPORTUNITY

Which areas should you look at first? After all, it would be difficult to sort through hundreds of outsourcing arrangements and find the critical few. One way to start is to review the Ten Ailments outlined in chapter 3 to identify those areas/contracts that are causing the most pain. These ailments may begin to highlight areas where both the customer and the service provider can gain the most from a Vested Outsourcing agreement. Why? Simply put, fighting ailments takes energy; it can be emotionally and financially draining. Both organizations are expending resources to mitigate the impact of the ailment.

If Vested Outsourcing looks promising for the opportunity you have identified, the next step is to dig a bit deeper. Key questions include:

- Is my organization capable of functioning in a Vested Outsourcing environment?
- What am I attempting to accomplish, especially in terms of cost and service levels?
- What is the desired outcome?
- Who will be impacted?

Understanding the opportunity is part of laying the foundation. If you cannot answer these questions, you should not proceed further until you can, as everything is dependent on them. Poor foundations lead to poor structures—whether in buildings, contracts, or relationships. We will look at these questions in more detail as we proceed in this chapter.

Do You Know What Your Organization Is Designed to Do?

Many companies that outsource have followed Tom Peters's advice: "Do what you do best and outsource the rest."[1] However, our experience shows that companies often fall into the outsourcing paradox and fail to let their service providers be the experts. In a conventional outsourcing environment, the emphasis is on conformance to contract requirements and adherence to contract terms. Little incentive, leeway, or opportunity is offered for service providers to explore innovative approaches. In fact, in many cases, there are significant disincentives to creativity, many resulting in the activity trap ailment discussed in chapter 3. All too often the emphasis is on compliance, not continuous or transformational improvements. Moreover, service providers that introduce new ideas may encounter significant obstacles, requiring complex, costly, and often painful contract modifications.

In a compliance-oriented environment, a service provider usually assigns its people clearly delegated authorities within a highly defined structure of roles, responsibilities, and accountabilities. This structure is a logical response to the customer's emphasis on compliance. The outsource provider finds a way to give the customer exactly what it contracted for and then locks in the structure to deliver it. You get what you asked for, not what you wanted. These environments usually do not support innovation or creativity, as it is not on the organizational chart.

In a Vested Outsourcing environment, the emphasis is on new approaches, on continuous improvement methodologies, and on driving to find a better way of doing things. Vested Outsourcing encourages a creative quest to deliver improved performance outcomes, effectiveness, and value. As a result of these efforts, both the company outsourcing and the service provider share in the improvements.

This emphasis on innovation goes to the very heart of the company: its culture. Edgar Schein, Sloan School of Management professor at the Massachusetts Institute of Technology, defines organizational culture as "the residue of success" within an organization. According to Schein, culture is the most difficult organizational attribute to change, outlasting products, services, founders and leadership, and all other physical attributes of the organization. Companies that outsource and service providers that established themselves in a legacy-thinking world have a residue of success, but it looks nothing like the culture required in a Vested Outsourcing world.[2]

Organizations contemplating a shift to Vested Outsourcing need to ask themselves—and their service providers—whether their structure and organizational culture will foster the shift. Answering the next series of questions will help you to decide whether you are ready or not.

How Suitable for Vested Outsourcing Is the Service Being Outsourced?

Many services can be managed successfully with or without a Vested Outsourcing business relationship. The key issue is to understand the suitability of the requirements for your organization's experience level.

What would be the difference between using the Vested Outsourcing process and conventional outsourcing? One key determinant will be the Pony. How much money can you save by working together? How can the two companies become more efficient? The larger the Pony, the better the opportunity for Vested Outsourcing. Remember that this is hard work, and firms will have to go through a lot of manure to uncover the Pony. The effort has to be worthwhile.

Another consideration is the size and stability of the overall value of the work that is outsourced, often referred to as the book of business. An organization just starting out with Vested Outsourcing should select a stable, well-understood service area for the initial program: facilities management, maintenance, logistics services for established businesses, and the like. There is less risk associated with a well-established service area that has been in operation for several years with a solid history of cost and performance.

Service areas that can be improved by process and technology innovation are often good candidates for Vested Outsourcing, as they typically have a larger potential Pony. For example, recall that General Electric helped bring Lean and Six Sigma thinking to the U.S. Navy, dramatically improving the Navy's engine maintenance program for the F/A 18 Hornet program. And Grubb & Ellis brought both process efficiencies and cost-saving ideas to Microsoft.

How Suitable Is the Relationship?

Just because there is a Pony does not mean you should go for it. Relationships matter. If there are concerns about long-term trust, ability to work together, or a lack of buy-in on continuous improvement on either side of the table, the Pony may be unattainable. Worse yet, it could be obtained but the results not shared as originally agreed.

How do you know if the relationship will work? Ask yourself:

- How well do you trust each other?
- How often are there problems?
- When there is a problem (and there are always problems in any relationship), how is it handled? Is everyone treated fairly?
- How open is the relationship? Does everyone share information?
- How long have we all worked effectively together? (The longer, the better.)

You Are Experienced, but Do You Have the Right Experience?

Most firms have not done full Vested Outsourcing agreements but some firms have done parts of the process. Many firms are strong in spend analysis, market research, or understanding customer needs. Some have experience in offering incentives for performance and know how to define and measure outcomes. However, having an open and sharing culture is probably one of the most important attributes in a Vested Outsourcing relationship because so much is based on driving innovations that bring mutual benefits to all parties involved. Recall economist Robert Solow's study on the impact of innovation, which he termed *technical change*. Technical change was defined as improvements in business process or improvements in products, driven by innovation. Solow concluded that 87 percent of economic growth could be explained by technical change, or the brainpower to create innovative solutions.[3]

All of these questions tie to the critical foundation on which the Vested Outsourcing agreement will rest. These experiences shape how firms approach an opportunity and solve a problem. They shape how firms view the world, and the other firms and individuals in it.

IT IS ABOUT COMMITMENT

More than anything else, Vested Outsourcing is a partnership between a company and a service provider. The partners must understand Vested Outsourcing and must commit to the process and to each other. Vested Outsourcing is not gainsharing or just a tweak of the status quo; it fundamentally transforms and realigns the business relationship.

How long is the commitment? Most arrangements we have seen are for 3- to 5-year contracts, although we have seen contracts up to 20 years. The commitment is long term, regardless of the risks, regardless of the uncertainty. A Vested Outsourcing arrangement must accept uncertainty and risk and then manage through it. "All for one, one for all" does not come with an expiration date.

DIG THE FOOTERS

One of the significant decisions to be made is how to select a partner for a Vested Outsourcing initiative. On one hand, it makes sense to partner with a supplier with whom you have a relationship or track record. By doing so, you minimize the time necessary to develop rapport and trust, as time and experience are on your side.

Another option is to select the project and then look for potential service providers. A major difference between Vested Outsourcing and a more standard strategic sourcing approach is the early involvement of potential partners, particularly when circumstances dictate a competitive bid for the work. One way to identify potential suppliers is through thorough market research.

Which method is best? If you are just starting, we recommend teaming with a current service provider or customer on a project that has a Pony. If, however, your culture is fairly open and you have a proven history of selecting strong partners, "dating" before making a final selection can definitely work. Both approaches have benefits—and risks—that have to be understood and managed. And that understanding comes from a cross-functional team working together to find the Pony.

FORM THE TEAM

For managers raised in a cost-plus world, Vested Outsourcing is a radical change. It creates a world of opportunity in revenue and profit growth for the service provider. For the company outsourcing, it also carries the assumption of responsibilities that are new and different, and may entail significant risk. Not all organizations are ready to step into Vested

Outsourcing, which fundamentally transforms behavior by shifting the focus to outcomes instead of activities. A comparable shift is required in organizational culture and capability, and risk tolerance must be considered.

A good Vested Outsourcing team working to select a service provider consists of a cross-functional group made up of the process owners of the company outsourcing and key stakeholders and users of the process. One of the first things to understand is the roles and responsibilities of the key players in a typical Vested Outsourcing program. It is not absolutely necessary to have every player represented on the team from Day 1. The team should be developed with the program and the desired outcomes in mind, and players should be added at the appropriate time. Next we outline and define some of the roles typically associated with sound Vested Outsourcing.

Program Manager

The responsibility of the program manager (PM) is to develop and implement Vested Outsourcing strategies that will ensure the desired outcomes at the optimal cost to the company that is outsourcing. The PM has primary responsibility for every aspect of the life cycle management of the program. It is the PM's job to work with the customer stakeholders to determine desired performance outcomes. The PM is then responsible to develop relationships, contracts, and performance goals with service providers to ensure that those goals are met. The PM ultimately is responsible for the success of the program and the attainment of the specified goals, and is the person who will authorize payment for the work performed.

Process Owners/Users/Customers

The process owners are the subject matter experts of the team and the true customers of the service being outsourced. Although they might not be able to express concisely the desired outcomes, they are the ones who will feel the pain most severely if the service provided is less than satisfactory. Their viewpoints may appear myopic at times and distorted at others, but they must be fully explored until understood. During this exploration, it is often useful to use the Five Whys technique for root cause analysis. Ask process owners to describe the pain or problem, and then ask: "Why is this a problem?" Continue to ask "Why?" until you get past the symptoms to the underlying causes of the problem.

This questioning will expose an issue for the service provider to address when creating the solution. By the way, it helps to let process managers know the nature of the technique being used; otherwise, the situation can become very contentious.

Sourcing

In a normal outsourcing project, the sourcing group pretty much goes it alone, but in Vested Outsourcing, that group has help from the rest of the team. The sourcing group's role does not change significantly, however. It searches out sources, arranges visits, coordinates the flow of information between company and suppliers, and in general performs all normal sourcing duties. The major difference is the shift away from the activity focus to a results or outcome focus. This difference can be significant for experienced sourcing people making the shift to Vested Outsourcing, so the rest of the team must be cognizant and supportive in helping the sourcing people adjust to this new method.

Contracting

It is important not to underestimate the importance of the role of contracting in a Vested Outsourcing program. Contracting is responsible for documenting the contract requirements and ensuring that there is fair competition leading to a contract. Contracting people usually have the least amount of knowledge and experience when it comes to Vested Outsourcing and should be brought into the process as early as possible; failure to include the contracting group from the beginning may set the Vested Outsourcing process back.

Senior Management and Stakeholders

As things begin to get organized, it is critical to ensure the involvement and support of senior management. Research conducted by McKinsey confirms that there is a direct correlation between senior leadership involvement and project success.[4] It is not necessary to have every one of these senior stakeholders on the core team, attending every meeting. But every project phase concludes with a review meeting or gate to the next phase. Think of these senior stakeholders as the gatekeepers, and consider carefully the price of admission to pass through each gate. In Vested Outsourcing, as in life, it helps to know the price in advance before requesting admission through to the next level. We examine stakeholder analysis in more detail a little later.

Additional Team Members

Finally, at various stages in the project, additional members will need to be added to the team—sometimes on a temporary basis, sometimes for the duration. These would include, but not be limited to, cost/price analysts, quality assurance, legal, and finance. As the team plans each phase, it is important to review the membership continually and adjust the team as necessary.

One additional team member to be added who is unique to Vested Outsourcing is the supplier. It is critical that suppliers are involved with the identification of the Pony and also understand the needs of all the stakeholders. Allowing them an opportunity to listen to the dialogue helps them to put the needs into context.

You might be thinking that allowing a supplier into these meetings is like asking the fox to guard the henhouse. With all of this information, you may argue, the service provider will understand our points of pain, internal deliberations, and use that against us, either in defining what it will provide us or in determining the rates it will charge.

That is a legitimate fear. And, if it is present, it may suggest that you have not selected the right potential partner for the project. As an analogy: If I tell my best friend some of my problems, am I concerned that she will use it against me when she has a chance? What type of friend is that?

Reality has to take both extremes into perspective; we discuss this a bit more in a few pages. Certainly the service provider should not be involved in each and every decision. Some decisions and discussions are internal deliberations. Yet you must begin to draw back the curtains to allow a greater dialogue so that you *and* the service provider share information to get the Pony.

POURING THE FOUNDATION

Once you have established the team, its members will need to work on the activities that will find the Pony. Next we present a brief overview of each activity.

Project Planning

A good cross-functional team will have awareness of the entire project. However, not every team member has the same degree of responsibility for project tasks. As the project plan is developed, it is important that the team members know what is expected from them. We recommend that you assign individuals a role for each task. This methodology is commonly known as RACI, as the roles are:

- Responsible. This is the person who actually does the work to achieve the task. Multiple resources can be responsible for doing the work on a large task, so best practice is to divide the work into component parts so that one person is responsible for each component.
- Accountable. This is the person who ultimately is answerable for the correct and thorough completion of the task. There must be only one *A* specified for each task, following the common wisdom that if two people are accountable, then no one is.
- Consulted. These are the people whose opinions and contributions are sought to complete the task. Two-way communication is critical, with information offered and evaluated openly.
- Informed. These people must be kept up-to-date on progress. In general, this is one-way communication, unless they respond with an objection or inquiry.

A project plan developed with a RACI method might look something like that the three tasks shown in Figure 6.2.

Develop each team with the program and the desired outcomes in mind. As the project plan is fleshed out, take care to properly align the workload with the team members, utilizing their skills and experiences but not overloading anyone. As in all well-managed projects, the team also should spend the time developing its rules of conduct, vision statement, and charter. Members should make provisions to update regularly their project plan, projected timeline, key tasks, action items, and schedule constraints. As these activities are common to all well-managed projects, it is unnecessary to discuss them in further detail.

As the RACI shown in Figure 6.2 indicates, Bill has to identify the stakeholders. Beth is accountable if he fails, or if the output does not meet the team's needs. Why put Bill's name on the RACI? No name, no commitment. Teams typically are most ineffective when members can be anonymous. In such situations, blame is shared

Figure 6.2   Vested Outsourcing Project Plan

	Duration	Due	R	A	C	I
Conduct stakeholder analysis						
Identify stakeholders	2 days	3/11	Bill	Beth	Pete Sam	Kris
Identify insights, interests, and objectives	2 days	3/13	Sam	Beth		
Identify issues and objections	3 days	3/14	Sam	Beth	Team	

and responsibility is ignored. By clearly articulating who is responsible for an outcome, team members can be held accountable for the results.

UNDERSTAND THE NEED: STAKEHOLDER ANALYSIS

At this stage, it is important to recognize who the stakeholders are and engage them in the process. A stakeholder is anyone who has an interest in the success of an organization in delivering intended results and maintaining the viability of its products and services.[5] It is important to name names when recognizing your stakeholders. Do not say "Marketing"; instead, identify the individual who will be the primary decision maker in that department, even if it is not the person that the department "assigned" to the project.

Stakeholder Ranking

All stakeholders are important, but some have higher stakes in the process. You should rank them in order of importance to your program, recognize their needs, and work closely with them to address their concerns. After you have identified the stakeholders, analyze their power based on their influence and their importance.

Influence can be defined as the extent to which a stakeholder is able to act on project operations and therefore affect project outcomes. This is a measure of the stakeholder's power. Key factors include his or her control over the project funding and extent to which he or she informs decision making around investments in technology and workplace productivity. *Importance* is defined as the extent to which a stakeholder's problems, needs, expectations, and interests are affected by project operations or desired outcomes.

The overall power score is simply a product of the importance and influence scores. Figure 6.3 summarizes an example of the respective power positions of a project's stakeholders.

Due to their importance and influence, certain individuals or stakeholders will be key or primary stakeholders for the project as a whole. Without their explicit support or involvement, it is unlikely that the project can be concluded successfully.

Insights and Concerns

The next step in stakeholder analysis is to study their current position with regard to the proposed project. Start by listing the insights and concerns that your top-ranked shareholders have shared. Note: In some cases, stakeholders may be incorrect in their assessments; nevertheless, if that is their perception, you should list it, because you will have to deal with it! Consider what constitutes success from their perspective. Does the current product/service satisfy their needs? If not, why not? State this as specifically as possible. Is the current level of performance

Figure 6.3   Stakeholder Importance

	Low INFLUENCE	High
IMPORTANCE High	**Higher Importance** **Lower Influence: SECONDARY** **(score: 2)** Communications Director Procurement Director Marketing Director Individual Employees	**Higher Importance** **Higher Influence: PRIMARY** **(score: 4)** Chief Executive Chief Operating Officer Chief Financial Officer HR/Diversity Director
IMPORTANCE Low	**Lower Importance** **Lower Influence: OTHER** **(score: 1)** Peripheral Support Groups External Suppliers	**Lower Importance** **Higher Influence: SECONDARY** **(score: 2)** IT Director Line Managers
	Low **INFLUENCE**	High

satisfactory, or is a service level improvement required? Would they be satisfied with less if you could gain a price/cost advantage by lowering expectations in specific areas? In short, what are they complaining about?

Be sure that the communications plan specifically addresses these primary stakeholders and their concerns, and develop your strategy for communication accordingly. To assist you in this process, we have developed a stakeholder analysis tool. To download a copy, please visit www.VestedOutsourcing.com/resources and select *Stakeholder Analysis.*

RESEARCH THE POTENTIAL: MARKET RESEARCH

You have started to define where to find the Pony; the team is beginning to take shape. The issues are coming into clearer focus, as are possible alternatives and solutions. Market research is critical, and time consuming, as it will leverage the knowledge of others, not just team members. Do not skimp on market research time, and involve the whole team in gathering this critical information.

Before starting, make some careful decisions on who will do what by when. Avoid missteps by having a clear plan that identifies potential data sources and research methods, firms or individuals to interview, requests for information/questionnaires, literature searches, and the like. A wide perspective on the scope of information needed will yield dividends down the road. You will judge how to apply the data to the particular Pony later in the process.

One of the best ways to gather information is through site visits or interviews. Although there has been a significant amount of literature on how to perform such visits correctly, a few points are worth highlighting.

First, do your homework. Do interviews after you have completed an initial market scan, so that the team has a better grasp of the issues. The team also needs to research the firm it is visiting and to understand the unique opportunities it faces. The potential service provider's company leadership, vision, commitment, and support should also be considered.

Second, develop the team's questions into a standardized interview guide, considering the information that is required and therefore the questions that should be asked. Consider who will be interviewed and who will conduct interviews. Be sure to include leading questions, not those that can be answered by yes or no. Decide what the team will do with the answers before you ask the question, as this may influence the manner in which you decide to collect, document, and disseminate the information.

Potential suppliers can help determine what is possible. Try to move beyond the request for information (RFI) stage as early as possible, as one-on-one meetings are more effective than presolicitation or preproposal conferences. We have found it very effective to focus on industry best practices, performance metrics and measurements, innovative delivery methods for the required services, and incentive programs that providers have found effective. In addition, when talking with potential service providers, be sure to identify their capabilities and address quality assurance as well as financial vitality. Also try to identify recent innovations in technology and/or process.

Third, let suppliers help solve the problem. In many cases, they know what you do not know that you do not know. We will emphasize this important point again and again. Involve them in the process, and solicit their help.

For example, a Japanese grocery chain had a problem. The square footage in their stores is very limited and they do not have room to waste. Watermelons are big and round, and take up a lot of space. When customers take watermelons home, the fruit dominates the smaller Japanese refrigerators. Some suppliers might tell the grocery stores that there is nothing that can be done about it; as a result, few watermelons would be stocked in the stores and sold.

But some Japanese farmers took a different approach.[6] If the supermarkets wanted a space-efficient watermelon, they asked themselves, "How can we provide one?" It was not long before they developed the square watermelon!

The solution to the problem was not difficult for those who did not assume that the problem was impossible. As the watermelons grew, each was placed in a uniform square box; when the watermelons filled the boxes, they were ready for harvest. Stores could stock these watermelons in quantity, and shipments were easier and more cost effective. Consumers loved them because they took up less space in their refrigerators, meaning that growers could charge a premium price for them.

How does this anecdote apply to you on your journey to find the Pony? Here are a few lessons to take away from this story that may help you in all parts of your life:

- Don't assume that what is is what shall be in the future.
- Question habits.
- Creative trumps the status quo.
- Always look for a better way.
- Impossibilities usually exist in our thoughts, not in the realm of the possible.

WHERE DO YOU GO FROM HERE?

Gathering this information sets the foundation. Analyzing it and gaining perspective from it is the critical part. Think of the process as a giant funnel with a sieve at the bottom. You pour in all of the information, then shake it around to sort out the key pieces of wisdom and data that you need to move forward. Certain things are a given, such as the need to:

- Analyze the market for emerging suppliers and services.
- Identify key industry cost drivers.
- Identify benchmark costs for commodity products.
- Identify benchmark labor costs for commodity services.

Other areas are less obvious and are linked to your specific requirements. The better you can define your need before you start, the more efficient you will be in your research. But the flip side is that you do not know what you do not know. So be sure to look back, determine if additional research is needed, and allow time to gather the additional information.

When you have identified one or more high-potential service partners through your market research, the next step is to integrate them into the team. If you have identified a single partner, this integration is fairly simple, especially if that company is already providing the service to you. But it is also quite possible to involve multiple potential companies in the Vested Outsourcing process. The key is communication and clarity of expectation.

Finally, gather all of this information together, review it as a team, and communicate it to your key stakeholders. It is time to pass through the gate to the next phase, but your gatekeepers will want to see some results before turning you loose again. Be prepared to review your team vision and objectives, your market research report, and your plan for using this information to achieve your stakeholders' goals, thereby addressing their key issues and concerns.

CHECKLIST OF KEY DELIVERABLES— LAY THE FOUNDATION

- Roles and responsibilities
- Project plan
- Stakeholder analysis
- Communication plan
- Market research report

CHAPTER 7

UNDERSTAND THE BUSINESS

The initial step in the Understand the Business phase is to establish the baseline by documenting the as-is state of the current process being outsourced. A good baseline will help establish the desired outcomes, the single most important part of Vested Outsourcing. It is also the starting point for establishing the business case to justify the change financially and for developing contracts and agreements. A good baseline will provide a solid understanding of improvement opportunities and help to identify what the cost of a program will be—a key for any service provider signing up to take risk under a Vested Outsourcing agreement.

ESTABLISH THE BASELINE

Although some programs have such poor levels of performance or cost structures that a service provider could sneeze and make improvements, it is important for all parties on the team to understand the current state of the program. You should establish the baseline early on, prior to determining process improvement and redesign strategies. Do this well before developing the final contract because outsource providers will use this baseline to help them define the Pony.

The company outsourcing and the service provider can both participate in the baselining efforts equally. It is important to assess any knowledge gaps and communication barriers between the partners. The role of the service providers in baselining is to push for an objective, comprehensive, fact-based description of the current process. Good service providers are team players and may even drive the effort in coordination with their customers. If the company outsourcing wants to take a more hands-off approach, it still will need to provide service providers with the data and special resources needed to help establish a baseline, including access to interviews with current employees, existing process flows and cost data, volume data, and other information.

Many companies focus their baseline to capture the average volumes and simple activity costs associated with the work to be done. We have found that it is much better to follow three steps to ensure a comprehensive baseline.

1. Determine the scope.
2. Document the current state.
3. Identify potential opportunities.

Determine the Scope

Before the effort really begins, ask some tough questions. Doing so will help to make sure you are headed in the right direction. The first series of questions is pretty basic: What is the service you are sourcing, and why are you sourcing this service at this time? What is driving the process? What do you need? And perhaps most important, how will you know it is good when you get it?

That last question is critical to Vested Outsourcing because it determines how to measure the desired outcomes of the effort. The desired outcomes are the focal point of the effort—the primary message that you will communicate to the supplier and your stakeholders. Make sure you can answer that question before you proceed too far.

In order to help you, here are some additional details to ponder: What do you expect to improve over previous contracts or internal efforts? Service level? Cost? Availability? How are you sourcing the service today? Does it satisfy the customer? If not, why not? What alternatives have you considered in the past? How recently?

To demonstrate this concept of desired outcomes, we will compare four companies that reviewed the effectiveness of their in-house food services, but from very different perspectives.

The first was a high-technology firm, the second was an international headquarters located in a metropolitan area, the third was a headquarters of an industrial manufacturer, and the fourth was Google. Each of the four had a very different strategy for cafeteria management.

The goal for the high-tech firm was to reduce the cost of operating the food service facility. In the past, the facility had been highly subsidized, and the goal was to reduce overall operating costs in order to reduce or eliminate the subsidy.

For the metropolitan area headquarters, the goal was to increase employee productivity. The company wanted employees to stay on campus for lunch. It measured the lost productivity when employees traveled off-site and calculated 20 minutes a day could be saved by keeping them on campus; that equates to 80 hours over one year. But to do so, the company had to make the cafeteria attractive to employees.

The industrial manufacturer was seeking lower healthcare costs. Its studies had proven that healthy employees are less expensive to insure. In addition, they also take fewer sick days, are more alert at work, and therefore have increased productivity. This company wanted a menu that was more balanced and would lead to lower costs but again was attractive to employees. The company also combined the cafeteria program with a fitness program benefit.

One part of Google's strategy was to attract the best available employees. A way to ensure employee satisfaction is to offer free food from top gourmet chefs. Google's strategy was focused on having overall working conditions that ensure the company the pick of the best talent available.

Although all four companies were evaluating the effectiveness of their food service operations, each had a different desired outcome, or expectation. As a result, the definition of success for each would be very different. The metrics used to define success would vary from reducing healthcare costs to employee satisfaction, to increased hours at work. Understanding the desired outcomes impacts not only what has to be done but the size of the Pony.

This is why defining the scope of the project matters. If outsourcing involves a business process, there is usually a defined beginning and end. Where in your process will you hand off from internal process to the service provider? What information will be provided, and what information will the supplier have to obtain, and from where? When will the provider hand back the service or process to you, and what will that look like or entail? What systems will be shared? What systems will the supplier have to provide?

If what is being outsourced is not a business process but facility maintenance or food service, for example, defining the parameters is more critical. The scope should be defined at the activity level, not by the specific tasks. For example, if food service is being outsourced, what does it include? Catering? Vending? Who is responsible for equipment maintenance, or purchasing new equipment? The list continues, but make sure you consider the overall activity in terms of the *results* you seek, not the individual tasks that must be performed to achieve those results.

One common misconception is that a baseline simply captures the existing costs and key performance metrics for a program. That is only part of what we recommend. As discussed in earlier chapters, one key characteristic of a Vested Outsourcing business model is creating a business environment that holds service providers accountable for the activities that are required to deliver a certain performance level at a specified price. For this reason, we highly encourage development of a baseline that goes beyond simple cost and performance data to state the entire scope of what the service provider will be asked to take on—*including understanding key supply chain processes and activities for which service providers will assume responsibility.* In food service, that might include trends in utilization by employees, a monthly forecast of catering and special events, and existing equipment maintenance calendars. Consider including in the baseline anything that the potential supplier will need to understand about your current situation and your desired outcomes.

What Is the Scope of Your Partnership?

As with any significant change, stakeholders often disagree on the level of what should be outsourced. Not only is there usually a debate within the firm that is outsourcing; there usually also is a big difference between what the company that is outsourcing and the service providers feel is the correct level of service. One reason is that in many companies, employees fear job loss. Simply put, the more that is outsourced, the more jobs that will be lost. We like to think of it as not that jobs are lost but that jobs are *allocated to the right organization to perform that work.* Over time, the overall solution is improved so that jobs are reduced (possibly through attrition) until the right number of people are performing at the optimal level.

Often newcomers to the process believe that Vested Outsourcing agreements are the solution to all internal challenges. There is a common misconception that companies involved in Vested Outsourcing partnerships outsource all aspects of a particular function. That is simply not the case. We have seen successful Vested Outsourcing programs that range the gamut of scope.

A key point to remember is that the broader the scope of the program, the more risks the service provider is challenged to take on. In addition, the core desired outcomes and metrics used to define the service provider's success will change with the scope of its responsibility.

Baseline with a Purpose

To establish your baseline, identify current performance and opportunities. That includes performance (metrics), process gaps and/or opportunities, and current costs. In order to fully answer the question posed earlier—what do you expect to improve?—you must identify your as-is state. Where are you today? The most widely accepted process improvement methodology in practice today is commonly called Lean. Lean starts with the process mapping of the value chain, which is a fancy way of asking: how does the work get done today?

Understanding the process starts with detailing and validating the process customer's requirements. For instance, in the current process, how does the work get done? Who does it? Where and when does it get handed off from one individual or group to the next? Properly documenting the current process for acquiring commodities and/or services can be a tedious challenge, and often is met with significant resistance. There will be those who view this as a complete waste of time: "Why should we do this? We know we want to change them." But a thorough understanding of the current state will pay large dividends and eliminate a lot of false starts and blind alleys. That said, spend as little time as possible capturing roughly 80 percent of the detail—do not even try for 100 percent. Then look at how well the process performs today. Figure 7.1 presents an example of such a process map, followed by a brief analysis of the strengths, weaknesses, and opportunities for this process in Figure 7.2.

Figure 7.1   Process Map

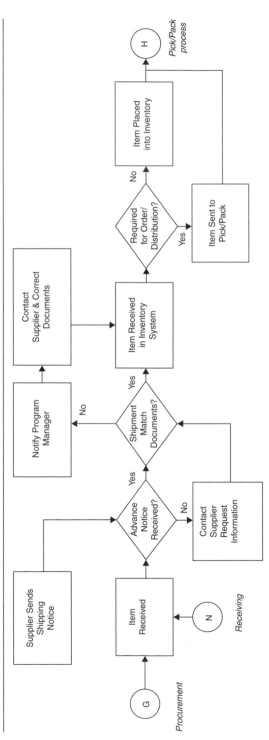

Figure 7.2   Process Analysis

Strengths	Weaknesses	Opportunities
All areas have inventory management systems in place Well managed receiving processes	Advance ship notice is not received on all shipments No notice that item has been released prior to receipt; SKU is not in the fulfillment house system Items in the shipment arrive with different product/item number from what is expected Some shipments arrive without adequate carton marking Pallet configurations not standardized (often do not meet fulfillment house requirements) Overages from printer distributions may arrive without advance notice	Standardize advance shipment notice process (e-mail notice is fine) Standardize product release process Standardize carton labeling to include product ID in barcode format; all cartons should be labeled Standardize pallet configuration through supplier shipping standards and education Improve printer drop shipment process

To build the process map, talk to the people who are actually doing the work. We find it best to do this where they work, not in a conference room. Interviewing in their workplace will help avoid misunderstandings in terminology and nomenclature. Ask the individual, "How do you...?" Before you even record the answer, ask, "Can you show me...?" By direct observation, you can use your own terms and gain a more complete understanding of the actual work.

Seek out the lead workers—experienced individuals who actually perform the work; avoid interviewing the manager/supervisor. On more than one occasion, we have interviewed the lead worker and manager at the same time. When asked "How do you...?" we found that managers would launch into a very complete explanation of the steps in the process. Meanwhile, the lead worker would say something like "I wish it worked like that," and then tell you how it was really done. How the process is supposed to work and how the work actually gets done day to day are often very different. Whenever possible, it is also useful to collect examples of reports, job aids, and related information as references to share with the team.

Ideal interviewers are somewhat familiar with the process and understand the terminology and descriptions offered. But they should not fully describe the process themselves or put words into the mouth of the worker being interviewed. To be most effective, interviewers should collect current information at the actual process site (not from procedure notebooks, design manuals, etc.). Interviewers should start with a quick walk-through of the entire process, not for data collection but to gain an overview and have the proper context for the pieces. It is best to begin at the customer end and work your way upstream, as this allows you to ask critical questions related to the flow of information and gives you perspective for questions such as: How do you know what to work on when? Where do you get your information/supplies?

Draw the initial process maps by hand, in pencil, unless you are very familiar and comfortable with a process-mapping tool, such as Microsoft Visio. If multiple interviewers are working on different parts of a process, do not divide the process map into segments to be done by different people; do it all together! This will avoid gaps in understanding and help you highlight gaps in the process itself. Be aware and accept that the maps will not be perfect; perfection cannot be achieved from interviews and spot observations. But understand that the maps serve a purpose, and even incomplete ones are a valuable step in the overall process improvement. Gaps are acceptable, but what is documented must be accurate.

After you complete the process map, your next step is to evaluate the as-is. We recommend two ways to look at your current processes: a quantitative and a qualitative evaluation.

Document the Current State

The temptation to skip the step of identifying and documenting current performance levels is very strong. When pursuing a new program, most companies are motivated to take action rather than take stock. However, documenting current performance levels is critical; if you do not know where you currently are, you will not be able to figure out how to get where you need to be.

When you baseline your operational performance, we recommend a scope that includes both quantitative and qualitative approaches. For example, you should not only know the actual cycle time of the distribution process to fulfill a spare parts order (e.g., 48 hours), but you should know what differentiates a good distribution practice from a bad practice (e.g., inventory management, picking, kitting, shipping). We call the former a *quantitative* baseline and the latter a *qualitative* baseline. It is important to know both because qualitative improvements to a process drive improved quantitative results.

Benchmarking is "the process of comparing performance against the practices of other leading companies for the purpose of improving performance."[1] Although you need to know and document the current performance of the existing solution, you should also understand how this stacks up against what is considered good. When capturing as-is performance levels, we recommend that you take the time to compare those levels against benchmarking data. Although cost data might be hard to come by, performance benchmarking data is available. Good companies use benchmarking data to set the targets for their Vested Outsourcing agreements.

In addition to benchmarking performance data, a good baselining effort should evaluate current documented processes against suggested minimum standards and industry best practices. An outsource provider's objective is to improve specific processes and operations within the business. Assessing existing processes is an excellent way to ground the service provider in how well the process works at this time. Doing a qualitative process assessment enables the service provider to look behind the data to understand *how* the company is achieving its current service levels.

- Quantitative benchmarking demonstrates best *RESULTS*
- Qualitative benchmarking demonstrates best *PRACTICE*
- PRACTICE generates RESULTS

It is important to evaluate both quantitative and qualitative inputs because together they can provide the complete picture of the potential value of closing the gaps. For example, a Fortune 500 distributor was achieving on-time shipments in the best-in-class range of at least 99 percent. However, its quantitative benchmarking results also showed that it was experiencing high overtime rates and costs nearly double industry averages. When the company embarked on the qualitative phase of the benchmarking effort, its investigation showed that the company was muscling through the shipping and receiving functions with rudimentary processes. The company was able to target initiatives to improve efficiency while maintaining high service levels. The initiatives were focused on the following areas:

- Supply demand alignment
- Inventory management
- Management of suppliers
- Technology
- Measurement

In the first two years, the company achieved productivity gains of 23 percent driving over $1.7 million in annualized savings.

Quantitative Benchmarking

As we discussed, benchmarking is generally thought of as quantitative, using specific measures to compare one company or division to another. Start by documenting the measures that currently are being collected. You must also document the formula or definition by which they are calculated or defined in order to be able to compare to best-in-class sources. It will save time down the road also if you record the means by which the measures are collected (automated versus manual); if manual, be sure to note the level of effort required to ensure that the value of the measure exceeds the cost of obtaining it.

The next step is to decide what constitutes success. Consider the following reference from Lewis Carroll's *Alice's Adventures in Wonderland*, where Alice is asking the Cheshire cat for directions:

> "Would you tell me, please, which way I ought to go from here?"
>
> "That depends a good deal on where you want to get to," said the Cat.
>
> "I don't much care where," said Alice.
>
> "Then it doesn't matter which way you go," said the Cat.[2]

Your goal does not have to be based on best practice, especially if the measure is not critical to your business strategy. But the target value of the measure does have to satisfy the needs of the customer. There are essentially two different approaches to benchmarking:

1. Measuring your company's performance against your competitors' performance
2. Measuring your company's performance against your customers' expectations

Are your customers satisfied with the current level of performance? Does this process require a service-level improvement? Would they be satisfied with less in some areas, if you were able to give them a higher level in others (e.g., increase the lead time but reduce the variability)? What is the goal?

There are many different ways to get quantitative benchmarking data—however, most of them cost money or require you to contribute effort. The Warehousing Education and Research Council (WERC) and the American Productivity & Quality Center (APQC) are among two of the best-known not-for-profit resources today. WERC metrics are focused on warehouse management and are free to all paid members. APQC works on a collaborative survey basis, where each organization contributes its own performance data in order to access the collective data. APQC also operates on a fee basis, with a charge for each measure, for companies that are unable or choose not to contribute their data. In addition, APQC has recently partnered with the Council of Supply Chain Management Professionals (CSCMP) to align the second edition of the *CSCMP Supply Chain Process Standards* to APQC's Process Classification Framework (PCF) and APQC's benchmark metrics, which is discussed in the next section.

Figure 7.3 demonstrates a method of presenting the results from a quantitative benchmarking analysis. The numbers in the far right column represent the as-is state for the measures shown in the left-hand column. The black circles graphically depict where those values fall against the collective industry benchmarks. This particular table demonstrates a significant opportunity for a reduction in cash-to-cash cycle time (a common industry metric easily calculated for any public company from information found in public financial statements).

Figure 7.3   Quantitative Benchmark

MEASURE	Major Opportunity	Disadvantage	Average/ Median	Advantage	Best in Class	COMPANY
Cash-to-Cash Cycle Time	119 ○		63		38	103
Inventory Days of Supply	> 83 ○	55.2–83	30–55.2	15.4–30	< 15.4	85.29
Days Sales Out-standing	> 46.8	42–46.8 ○	31–42	25–31	< 25	45
Days Payable	> 30 ○	30–31	31–45	45–51.8	< 51.8	33
Returns as % Revenue	5%		1%		0.4% ○	0.19%
Annual Work Force Turnover	> 30%	17.4–30%	10–17.4% ○	3–10%	< 3%	10.16%

Qualitative Benchmarking

The lesser-known form of benchmarking is qualitative benchmarking, which consists of comparing the attributes or practices of a process against industry minimum acceptable and best practices. As stated earlier, although the tendency is to focus on quantitative measures, the underlying processes must be examined and changed if you are to have any hope of real improvement. You can drive the numbers temporarily using positive and/or negative incentives coupled with high vigilance, but sustainable improvements can be gained only with changes to the processes themselves.

To do qualitative benchmarking, use industry-known best practice studies and other available best practice information to assess your qualitative performance on key processes. The better-known sources include:

- APQC Best Practice Consortium Studies
- CSCMP *Supply Chain Process Performance Standards*

- *Harvard Business Review* case studies
- Warehouse Education Research Council "WERC Watch" case studies

The *Supply Chain Process Standards* assessment tool offers general guidelines on minimum standard and best practices. Process attributes are listed for each area along with descriptions of the suggested minimum standards and typical best practice for that process. By comparing the descriptions of the processes in the *Standards* to the practices found in their own companies, managers can determine their performance level and identify opportunities for process improvements in their supply chain.

In the example shown in Figure 7.4, the person conducting the assessment for the current order receipt and entry process found that only one of the bullet points applied to the process observed. And it was found in the Suggested Minimum Process Standard column. Following the guidelines in the *Standards*, the assessor rated this process as a "2"—falling below minimum standards.

The next step is to determine the processes that are most important to the company. This rating is unique to every company, based on its business strategy and cost/performance implications of each process to its customers. We have found that the best way to determine the strategic impact and cost/performance impact of each process is by bringing the key stakeholders together for a consensus discussion. Otherwise, different people will argue that each process is very important. Experience has proven that if everything is important, then by definition nothing is important. In Figure 7.5, we illustrate the results of such a consensus meeting in the Strategic Impact and Cost/Performance Impact columns.

A Total Rating value is then assigned based on those impacts, with High Impact rated as a "3." Therefore, if a process scored a High Strategic Impact and a High Cost/Performance impact, it would achieve a maximum Total Rating of "6." Add the current process ratings based on the assessor's interviews and scoring in the CSCMP *Standards*, with the black circle presenting the below-minimum scores, the half-white/half-black circle representing the achievement of minimum standards only, and the white circle representing significant elements of best practice. Process areas that were scored a "5" or "6" and a black circle were then selected as the focus for process improvement efforts.

Figure 7.4   Quantitative Assessment Example

	SUGGESTED MINIMUM PROCESS STANDARD	TYPICAL BEST-PRACTICE PROCESS
Establish Inventory Management Constraints	• All inventory decisions are made with full knowledge of relevant costs and associated risk. • Inventory turns tracked for monthly review and adjustment. Inventory levels are set at least twice a year. • Excess and obsolete inventory is reviewed regularly at the part number level.	• The inventory targets/days of inventory goals are reviewed and adjusted weekly/monthly based on product life-cycle, ABC throughput, and SKU variability. • 100% of total inventory is categorized—active, usable, excess, obsolete—for appropriate action. • A formal excess and obsolete (E&O) process is in place. Inventory is tracked monthly and aggressively reduced using industry appropriate methods (promotions, auctions, brokers, etc). • Disposal and aftermarket techniques are implemented to deal with obsolete, stale and damaged inventories. • A complete SKU review and rationalization exercise is performed on an annual (or more frequent) basis.

	Below Minimum		Meets Standard		Best Practice	
Establish Inventory Management Constraints			X			

Figure 7.5   Process Assessment Summary

Legend:
- ● High Impact 3
- ◐ Medium Impact 2
- ○ Low Impact 1
- ● High Gap
- ◐ Medium Gap
- ○ Low Gap

PROCESS	Strategic Impact	Cost / Perf Impact	Total Rating	Gap
Supply Chain Planning	●	●	6	●
Supply Demand Alignment	○	●	4	◐
Inventory Management	●	◐	5	○
Strategic Sourcing	●	◐	5	●
Supplier Management	○	○	2	●
Purchasing	◐	●	5	○
Inbound Material Management	◐	◐	4	◐
Product Engineering	◐	●	5	●
Partnership & Collaboration	●	○	4	●
Product or Service Customization	○	○	2	○
Manufacturing Infrastructure	◐	◐	4	◐
Manufacturing Processes	●	●	6	●
Distribution Processes	●	◐	5	○
Support Processes	◐	○	3	◐

Based on this prioritization, the team should focus on the specific improvements the company needs in order to achieve its objectives. In Figure 7.6, the team selected all of the suggested minimum standards and three of the best practices. This helped form the basis for the company's "to-be" strategy and part of the basis for its desired outcomes from the outsourcing process.

IDENTIFY POTENTIAL OPPORTUNITIES

Figure 7.7 represents an overall summary that we have found useful for presentation to key stakeholders and gatekeepers. It illustrates on one page the current "as-is" and the desired "to-be" state for a grouping of processes. In addition, the two processes targeted for best practice include a key metric for judging when that level has been attained. This summary provides a roadmap for the desired process improvements.

Two clarifications are needed at this point. In these figures, we have assigned objective, numerical values to subjective judgments. You must keep this in mind throughout the evaluation process. Just because the performance has a number does not make it an objective, verified quantity that would receive the same number from every assessor. These assigned performance values are still judgment calls. Assigning a value helps in the prioritization process and has proven to be very useful. But please remember that these values still represent subjective findings.

Figure 7.6   To-Be Process Goal

	SUGGESTED MINIMUM PROCESS STANDARD	TYPICAL BEST-PRACTICE PROCESS
Establish Inventory Management Constraints	• All inventory decisions are made with full knowledge of relevant costs and associated risk. • Inventory turns tracked for monthly review and adjustment. Inventory levels are set at least twice a year. • Excess and obsolete inventory is reviewed regularly at the part number level.	• The inventory targets/days of inventory goals are reviewed and adjusted weekly/monthly based on product life-cycle, ABC throughput, and SKU variability. • 100% of total inventory is categorized—active, usable, excess, obsolete—for appropriate action. • A formal excess and obsolete (E&O) process is in place. Inventory is tracked monthly and aggressively reduced using industry appropriate methods (promotions, auctions, brokers. etc). • Disposal and aftermarket techniques are implemented to deal with obsolete, stale and damaged inventories. • A complete SKU review and rationalization exercise is performed on an annual (or more frequent) basis.

Figure 7.7   Performance Roadmap

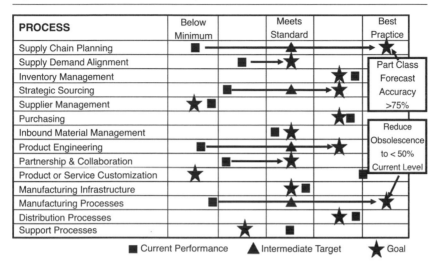

■ Current Performance   ▲ Intermediate Target   ★ Goal

The second clarification is in the area of best practice. People have a natural desire to be the best at everything. Objective analysis shows that this desire is not only virtually unattainable but also lacking in cost/benefit payoffs. Put simply, it costs too much to be the best at everything. We like the analogy of the decathlete. In the last two Olympic Games, the gold medal winners Roman Šebrle (2004 Athens) and Bryan Clay (2008 Beijing) finished first in only two and three events respectively. They both placed in the top five in seven events and shared one additional thing in common. They both placed dead last in the 1,500 meters, the last event in the competition. They both knew that all they had to do was finish the race to win the gold medal.

Sometimes all we need to do is complete a task—we do not have to be the best, we just have to meet the minimum standard for performance.

Most of this discussion has centered on companies assessing their own performance. If you are the supplier, what is your role in baselining the system? When you are the current supplier, it is especially important that you do your own independent data collection; you should not just accept the company's data but should compare the company's measures of your results to your own measures. The goal is to have objective and comprehensive facts in the system baseline. When you are not the current supplier, baseline your own performance for similar processes with other customers. Doing this will allow you to compare potential "to-be" scenarios and show your ability to help customers achieve the results they seek. Going forward, this baselining process also will help you work with the customer to establish:

- Desired metrics and incentives
- Alignment with your core competencies
- Alignment with your business investment opportunities
- An understanding of your associated risk levels

If you can show performance that is consistent with the customers' desired performance outcomes and corresponding metrics focused on their needs, along with systems that are operationally available, reliable, and effective, with a minimal logistics footprint and reasonable cost, you will be that much higher on the ladder of evaluation. Qualitative and quantitative baselining is a good place to shine and show you know best practice.

Establishing the Financial Baseline: Total Cost

It is critical that there is a shared understanding between company and supplier of the baseline costs. Baselining costs go beyond simply understanding the cost of the activities to be outsourced to the total operating costs spanning the organization. The outsource provider is being chartered to drive total costs down. Often the biggest improvement areas are in the handoffs between organizations. For this reason, it is critical to identify the cost of poor cross-functional performance and to target these costs for improvement. Figure 7.8 illustrates the importance of understanding total costs. Understanding only activity costs is just the tip of the iceberg. Often what is out of sight causes the greatest damage.

Conduct Spend Analysis

Spend analysis is a formal process for gathering the needed total cost information. The purpose of spend analysis is to identify how much is being spent, on what, from whom, for a specific commodity or service, across varying geographical/organizational units. Defined at its most

Figure 7.8   Total Cost of Ownership

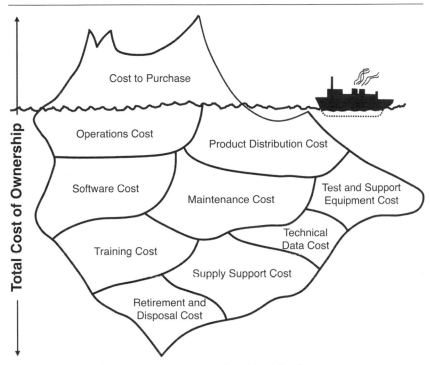

Source: University of Tennessee Performance-Based Logistics Courseware.

basic level, a spend analysis is an in-depth and fact-based study of an organization's procurement spend, with four key objectives:

1. Develop an organization-wide view of spend that is comprehensive, detailed, and accurate.
2. Identify opportunities for reducing total costs across the organization.
3. Establish a spend baseline against which to measure and compare future activity.
4. Prioritize initiatives for further analysis and implementation.

During development of the spend analysis, keep an additional purpose in mind: You must discover what potential suppliers need to know to size the effort required properly. Although Vested Outsourcing focuses on outcomes, not activities, spend analysis looks at the activities being performed today as the costs are being analyzed. This is very useful information for potential suppliers.

Spend analysis is best done following the 80/20 rule, which states that 80 percent of the total spend usually is contained in 20 percent of the total transactions. Poor-quality data, multiple naming conventions, and multiple sources are some of the problems you face when conducting spend analysis. Where possible, focus efforts on the data that can be obtained, and concentrate on the total cost of ownership for the transactions as a whole, with estimates filling the 20 percent gaps.

Establish the Desired Outcomes

Even though not all steps in the process must be carried out in order, you should develop desired outcomes only after you have understood the need and established the baseline. When developing performance outcomes, be sure to use corresponding metrics. The outcomes have to be objective and measurable, and the fewer, the better. The outcomes will become the foundation for the performance metrics that you will outline in the Statement of Objectives (SOO) and are indicative of what will be included in the contract in later stages. The desired outcomes are the key deliverables for which the service provider will be held accountable. Eventually you will translate these desired outcomes into the lower-level metrics that will be used to actually run the business.

High-level desired outcomes usually can be categorized as improvements to cost, schedule, and/or service/performance. The desired outcomes should be quantifiable and measurable, developed with the understanding that the stakeholders will value the change. Some example Vested Outsourcing desired outcomes are shown in Figure 7.9. It is for an agreement upgrading a company's buildings to be more energy efficient.

A successful Vested Outsourcing program requires focusing the project on the desired outcomes, or what you want the supplier to accomplish. Success is predicated on knowing the answers to two questions: What results do I need? and How will I know when I get them? The answers to these two questions are then used to align the SOO to the desired outcomes, including development of these areas:

- Performance objectives (aligning specific objectives to the desired outcomes)
- Performance standards (defining the measures of success)
- Performance inspection (ensuring delivery of success)

Figure 7.9   Exterior Lighting Example

Example Desired Outcomes
Energy conservation efforts that reduce headquarters carbon footprint by 20%
Cost management practices that reduce planned total campus facilities operations costs by 10%
Reduce energy consumption of exterior lighting by 50%
Provide a ROI that pays for the total cost of ownership within the estimated equipment life cycle (5 years)
Establish a standardized program that will provide the same ROI to all corporate sites where the energy cost exceeds X

A Statement of Objectives is very different from a standard Statement of Work. Briefly, a SOO describes the results, not the tasks. Based on the SOO, a supplier can draft a Performance Work Statement (PWS) that defines in more detail the work to be performed and the results expected from that work. In drafting the SOO, be very careful to let the supplier, not your company, solve the problem. Follow these guidelines:

- Do not write the objectives too tightly or too narrowly.
- Allow for and encourage creativity from the supplier.
- Be open to new solutions and new approaches.

Remember that how you write the Statement of Objectives will either allow innovative solutions or limit suppliers' ability to propose them.

The team is also responsible for developing a set of measures to determine if these outcomes have been met. By default, and necessity, they are high-level measures that are easily understood by business stakeholders and all parties involved in the process. Will you be interested in lower-level metrics? Yes, but these lower level metrics are more the early-warning measures that tell you whether the project is working appropriately or not. The supplier should be responsible for the lower-level operational metrics that support the higher-level business metrics. These lower-level metrics will clearly define the service level that the service provider is actually providing. Service providers must be careful not to agree to be held accountable for metrics that they do not manage or perform. In addition, be sure that you also consider the ability to collect and report on data pertaining to the metrics as part of this process, clearly specifying whether it is the responsibility of the company or the provider to collect and publish the data.

Some typical high-level sample performance measures for out-sourced logistics are those that are go beyond measuring simple activities and impact financial or customer performance:

Customer metrics
- First contact resolution rate
- Customer retention rate

Operational metrics
- Perfect order index

Financial metrics
- Cash-to-cash cycle time
- Distribution costs as a percent of sales

Employee metrics
- Annual turnover

Proper metrics should help drive performance to meet strategy, as shown in Figure 7.10. This alignment of performance is the reason that we work through the process of linking outcomes to strategy and measures to outcomes.

Figure 7.11 shows a situation where the measures are not properly aligned to the strategy. Performance will track against the measures—people are very good at understanding exactly how their performance will be measured and adjusting their methods and work habits accordingly.

When the measures are aligned to the strategy, the performance also will be aligned. It seems so simple; why do we get it wrong so often? Consider the next situation.

Figure 7.10   Performance Alignment

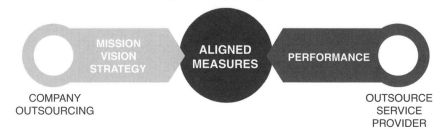

Figure 7.11   Performance Misalignment

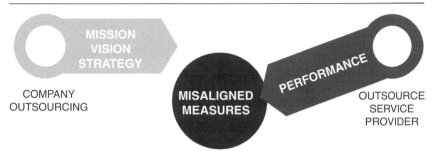

A large dairy processing company established performance measures and incentives for its employees. The procurement group was incentivized on purchase price variance—its ability to purchase material for less than the standard cost. Incentives in manufacturing centered on productivity as measured by machine utilization. Procurement sourced a key raw material at a price significantly below market cost. The low cost material passed all the specifications, so the procurement person bought a large quantity. However, this material could not be processed at the standard machine speed. The machines had to be slowed down, to the point where the additional manufacturing cost exceeded the raw material savings.

The procurement person got a bonus, but the manufacturing person was penalized and the company lost margin—all because the incentives were suboptimal, and not aligned to overall corporate strategy.

When developing the desired outcomes, first analyze the lessons learned from previous outsourcing or current in-house performance. This is why we stress the need to do baselining and benchmarking first. The goal is to identify areas of the current process that could be improved for efficiency, in cost, schedule, performance, or various combinations. Also, document the different strategies in use across the company or sometimes even at a single location. Is a difference in strategy driving different results? Can those differences be leveraged to optimize the overall results?

Another way to think of desired outcomes is as a need statement. Ask: What do we need? How can we align this need to our corporate mission and outcome goals? How can we provide the context to all team members to understand the impact that achieving these outcomes will have to the company? Once again, also ask these key questions: *Is outsourcing even needed?* Should we be performing this activity in house? What is the baseline—the current level of performance? What intermediate outcome issues must a potential supplier overcome?

In some cases, it will be difficult to establish precise measures using existing systems and methods of data collection. In those cases, you must weigh the expense of gathering the information against the potential value to be gained from it. Think about this observation from A. G. Lafley, former CEO of Procter & Gamble: "Simply because something can be counted doesn't mean it is worth counting. Count what counts despite the difficulty and imprecisions. Imprecise measurement of the right thing will tend to become precise measurement tomorrow."[3]

Once the team has defined the desired outcomes, subject those outcomes to critical thinking by your stakeholders and the world at large to make sure that you have agreement, and that you have not missed specific critical details. To do this, we recommend these steps:

- Contact potential vendors and industry peers for their perspective on your current processes.
- Contact the lead workers (the most experienced people who are actually doing the work) to review your findings for accuracy.
- Contact your stakeholders to gain an understanding of operational processes, to share your findings and gain their agreement.
- Communicate with management to gain their perspective and buy-in.

Well-defined and documented desired outcomes are critical to a successful Vested Outsourcing program and provide a strong framework for the rest of the process. Do not shortcut this step.

BUILD THE BUSINESS CASE: IDENTIFY THE PONY

Once the baseline assessment is complete and the desired outcomes are defined, the company and the service provider need to work together to identify performance opportunity areas they believe they can impact. A key part of this particular task is to identify any potential constraints. One such constraint may be an existing information technology system; for example, a logistics service provider might be required to integrate with the customer's order management system. The service provider will then refine the business case analysis with the goal of identifying the potential value of inefficiencies in the current solution. Under a Vested Outsourcing program, the service provider takes on the responsibility for delivering a certain level of performance at an agreed-on price. A good service provider will want to know going into the Vested Outsourcing arrangement where it will have quick-win opportunities to make improvements as well as where it may need to make longer-term investments.

This brings us to back to the Pony, the difference between the value of the current solution and the potential optimized solution. The Pony represents something that the outsourcing company wants but could not get on its own or with existing service providers.

Building the business case is key because it identifies the potential value of the Pony and helps determine the appropriate combination of service-level improvements and cost-savings. Both the service provider and the company outsourcing should use the Pony to determine the appropriate incentive levels to offer the service provider to achieve these improvements and savings. The bigger the Pony, the bigger the incentives the service provider should have the chance to earn.

If the outsource provider can capture the Pony and earn the incentives—say by achieving service-level and cost targets—everyone wins, because the outsourcing company finally gets what it wants. The catch: The company has to share the value of the Pony with the outsource provider that helped achieve it. The value of the Pony is used to fund the incentives for the outsource provider.

The methods for building and presenting a business case are as varied as the opportunities themselves. Key steps in the process are:

- Determine the cost savings of the proposed changes.
- Determine the performance improvements of the proposed changes.
- Determine the costs to implement the proposed changes.

Outsourcing providers have extensive experience in building business cases, and the team should leverage it. Let the supplier help build the case and show the gains for both teams.

This phase concludes with a stakeholder review. We firmly believe in a gated process, where your stakeholders are the gatekeepers. In your stakeholder analysis, you identified the people who needed to approve your progress and effectively give you permission to move forward. To conclude this phase, present your key work products to them, and gain their consensus and approvals. Exactly what you must present to whom will vary from company to company. The list below should be considered as advisory; add to or subtract from it as appropriate for your situation.

CHECKLIST OF KEY DELIVERABLES—
UNDERSTAND THE BUSINESS

- Scope of the effort
- Quantitative performance baseline
- Qualitative performance baseline
- Spend analysis: Desired outcomes
- High-level business case (the Pony)

CHAPTER 8

ALIGN INTERESTS

Now begins the transition from research to action. To this point we have focused on understanding the current situation, current processes, marketplace, and opportunities. Now it is time to begin planning how to create value by implementing process change and realigning workloads.

This stage entails designing and documenting how the outsourcing company and the service provider will work together to achieve the desired outcomes. It is the first pass at envisioning how the companies will interface to best achieve results. The current culture within the different organizations will be important, but the teams should be very careful that the easy path does not lead straight to various ailments, such as the outsourcing paradox, the junkyard dog factor, and/or the zero-sum game. Companies must give a certain amount of control to the service provider in order for the provider to overcome the inherent risks that come with the responsibility for ensuring the desired outcomes.

DEVELOP THE BUSINESS MODEL

When outsourcing various activities, it is important to understand how the various functional organizations will need to work together. A supply chain approach is often the easiest and most highly productive starting point for a phased acquisition Vested Outsourcing strategy. Because of the silo structure of many companies, often service providers can deliver performance improvements more rapidly through supply chain reengineering, Lean, or Six Sigma efforts than the company itself can achieve.

The process of integrating a new service provider into your business is much closer to hiring and training a new employee than it is to purchasing a commodity. The two companies need to build working relationships, bridges for communication and planning, to ensure that the mutual desires of both are realized. Even when the outsource provider already has been working for your company in a smaller role, enlarging that role is akin to promoting from within, and should receive the same care and attention. As A.G. Lafley of Procter & Gamble pointed out, "It's essential that manufacturers and retailers focus on joint value creation, joint business goals and plans, and joint responsibility for executing with excellence and delivering better business and financial results."[1]

Likewise, when outsourcing any business process, a good outsourcing business model will ensure the desired outcomes are achieved through proper allocation of resources and risks. Although we describe risk analysis here as a series of steps, it is really an ongoing effort that continues throughout the life cycle of the performance partnership.

WHAT IS YOUR RISK TOLERANCE?

There are known risks associated with outsourcing; indeed, many consider it a risky business overall. But that has not seemed to slow the trend. When risks go unidentified, or when a company elects to shift them to a service provider without a full understanding of the associated costs and potential outcomes, the relationship will labor under a substantial burden that it may not survive. This problem is even greater with the rise of multivendor outsourcing models.

Both the outsourcing company and the service provider must consider their tolerance level for risk. As mentioned, Vested Outsourcing is not for the faint at heart; the very backbone of Vested Outsourcing involves balancing risk and reward trade-offs that put pressure on the outsource provider to develop innovative and cost-effective solutions.

Two figures illustrate this point. Figure 8.1 illustrates a conventional outsourcing arrangement for a third-party logistics service. The company that outsources typically has a supply chain manager that performs many of the critical functions for its supply chain (even if these functions are not performed very well). A company might choose to outsource manufacturing, warehousing, returns, or all of the above.

Figure 8.1   Traditional Outsourcing

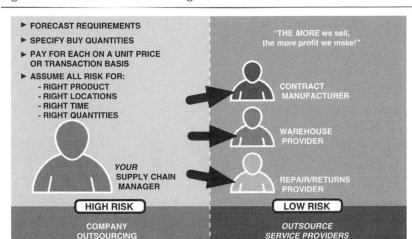

Under a typical transaction-based model, the more services the outsource provider sells the more revenue—and profit—they earn.

Under the traditional outsourced model, supply chain management typically develops a Statement of Work (SOW) and contracts with each service provider to perform the associated tasks within its SOW. The company that is outsourcing retains the risk of balancing supply and demand (the brainwork).

Under a Vested Outsourcing partnership, the company might recognize that it is simply not good at supply chain management activities and choose to outsource to a service integrator, which may or may not be one of the companies providing the actual outsourced services. This is depicted in Figure 8.2.

As Figure 8.2 illustrates, the company that is outsourcing focuses its efforts on identifying its desired outcomes and associated performance metrics. In this case, the company worked with a service integrator that took over all of the various aspects of managing its supply chain, and the service integrator/outsource provider bore the risk of achieving the company's desired outcomes.

In a properly structured Vested Outsourcing process, the outsource provider must be motivated to improve processes and reduce costs.

For some companies, Vested Outsourcing is simply too much of a risk to take on. But there is no innovation without risk. Opportunity

Figure 8.2   Vested Outsourcing

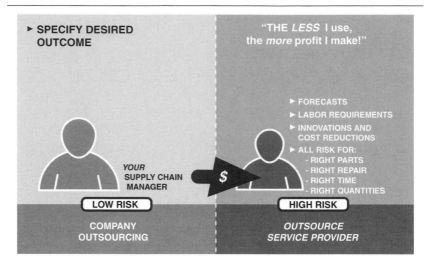

usually is accompanied by uncertainty. If it were not so, the change would have already been accomplished. Often a crisis of some sort is required to push companies to innovate, to take risks. Typical risk-related challenges we hear from companies just embarking on their Vested Outsourcing are outlined in Figure 8.3.

This is not to say that risks can't be managed. In fact, a properly structured and managed Vested Outsourcing program can mitigate virtually all of the risks shown in Figure 8.3. But before you can manage and mitigate risks, you have to identify and prioritize them. No shortcuts here!

Figure 8.3   Vested Outsourcing Risks

Company Outsourcing	Outsource Provider
We will lose control. I don't want to get locked into an outsource provider. What if the outsource provider fails? What if my costs turn out to be higher, or the service levels drop?	I don't want to take on risk when I know my customer won't change. When I deliver cost savings, they will just come back and hammer me for more. What if they do not keep me in the loop as demand changes?

CONDUCT A PERFORMANCE RISK ANALYSIS

The first step is to identify the risks. Murphy's Law is a good guide here, as anything that can go wrong probably will. Separate the project risks from the ongoing program risks, and deal with each category independently. The process is the same, but the timing and durations change significantly.

Some of the areas to be investigated include:

- *Business/programmatic risk.* Scheduling issues may impact success.
- *Technical risk.* Maturity of technology and processes reliant on technology must be assessed.
- *Funding risk.* Does access to funds rely on pending events or approvals? Have adequate funds been identified?
- *Process risk.* Do new processes have to be implemented?
- *Organizational risk,* such as the risk of implementing change within an organization.
- *Stakeholder risk.* Stakeholders change, or their needs change over time.
- *Risk summary.* Overview of the risk associated with implementing the initiative; for example, is there adequate service life remaining to justify this change?

When the risks are identified, categorize them according to "Likelihood" and "Severity" as shown in the descriptions in Figure 8.4 and Figure 8.5 respectively.

Figure 8.4   Risk Likelihood

Level	What is the likelihood that the event will occur?
A	Remote
B	Unlikely
C	Likely
D	Highly Likely
E	Near Certainty

Figure 8.5   Risk Severity

Level	Technical Performance... and/or	Schedule... and/or	Cost... and/or	Impact on Other Teams
1	Minimal or no impact	Minimal or no impact	Minimal or no impact	None
2	Acceptable with some reduction in margin	Additional resources required; able to meet needed dates	<5%	Some impact
3	Acceptable with significant reduction in margin	Minor slip in key milestones; not able to meet all needed dates	5–7%	Moderate impact
4	Acceptable; no remaining margin	Major slip in key milestone or critical path impacted	7–10%	Major impact
5	Unacceptable	Cannot achieve key team or major milestone	>10%	Unacceptable

Then you can prioritize risks by plotting the "Likelihood" and "Severity" according to Figure 8.6 to determine if the risk is high, moderate, or low.

When you have determined the risk level, you can formulate risk mitigation plans, with resources allocated as appropriate to the level of risk. To assist in this process, we developed the risk mitigation tool, illustrated in Figure 8.7. To download a copy of this tool, please visit www.VestedOutsourcing.com/resources and select *Risk Mitigation Tool.*

Figure 8.6   Risk Level

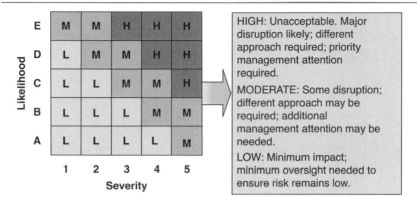

For each risk, it is important for you to state what actions are to be taken to reduce or eliminate the risk (the Mitigation Plan), state who is responsible for ensuring that those actions are taken, and set a target date for review. As mentioned earlier, risk mitigation is an ongoing process. The list of risks will change, with some being resolved and new ones being added. The severity of the risk also may change as new factors arise. Once risks are fully understood, appropriate decisions can be made to determine the level of risk that each partner faces.

DISTRIBUTE THE WORKLOAD

Distributing the workload is an important part of the process that is often misunderstood. In essence, it is the where, how, and by whom decision. Since total outsourced strategies are rare, it is important to find the right mix of work. The primary consideration is something we call the Best Value Assessment, which examines the capabilities, skills, infrastructure, and affordability of the company outsourcing and the alternative suppliers of the services to carry out the various subprocesses within the overall scope of work. In considering workload distribution, do not discount the "best value" potential of the people currently working for your company. Often significant business opportunities are associated with the use of an in-house facility and people. You have infrastructure, test equipment, facilities, and experienced workforces. In some cases, your people may have necessary training or even certificates or permits that can be

Figure 8.7 Risk Mitigation Example

Risk Description and Reason	Likelihood	Severity	Risk	Mitigation Plan	Responsible Party	Target Date	Status
Supplier may not have a clear understanding of the number of people required to accomplish the work within the Service Level Agreements (SLAs)	Likely	Moderate	Moderate	1. Staffing plan should include a buffer to mitigate staff attrition, ensure work is performed, and to cover temporary volume spikes. 2. The team structure and size will be constantly evaluated during and after the Transition Phase and adjusted as needed. 3. SLA penalites will not be enforced during the 90-day Post-Transition Phase.			
Insufficient documentation exists concerning certain jobs to assure that operational tasks are successfully executed	Remote	High	Moderate	Plan A: Training should incorporate support of all critical jobs and reporting. Plan B: During transition activities, trainers to ensure that the content needed is delivered and documented.			

	Near Certainty	Moderate	Unacceptable	Detailed communication plan to control all information flow, with all contractor contact to base run through Project Manager. Establish working relationships with all key stakeholders, early in the transition process.		
Staff may resist transition, especially if they lack confidence in successful transition and start-up						
Undocumented activities or higher level of support may be required beyond that documented in the Performance Work Statement (PWS)	Remote	Moderate	Minimal	1. Establish process to review Scope Changes in the weekly manager's meeting. 2. Establish process for large-scale impacts to be reviewed by Executive Steering Committee quarterly.		

difficult or costly for a service provider to obtain. Actual labor costs may be competitive or more than competitive. Understand both the required capabilities and the costs. In many cases, the service provider hires people who had been working for the company doing the outsourcing, and those people continue doing a version of their old job for a new employer.

BUILD THE REQUIREMENTS ROADMAP

The Requirements Roadmap, as shown in Figure 8.8, is a tool that we developed to organize the thinking and strategies associated with Vested Outsourcing. To download a copy of this tool, please visit www. VestedOutsourcing.com/resources and select *Requirements Roadmap*.

For Figure 8.8, we built upon the cafeteria example discussed in chapter 7. Everything is driven by the agreed-on desired outcomes, which go into the first column.

Since each desired outcome is rather broad, it is difficult to determine when or if you have achieved success. Therefore, each outcome is broken down into specific performance objectives that further define the various facets of each outcome, to be recorded in the second column. Two characteristics of these performance objectives are critical:

1. Avoid "how" words—describe the "what" and leave the "how" to the supplier.
2. Set fewer than five performance objectives for each desired outcome; otherwise, you will immediately begin to suffer from ailment 9, measurement minutiae.

The next two columns contain the standards that describe the measurement for each performance objective, and the acceptable quality level (AQL) describes the tolerance range, if any. There are times when the company has a target (say, 100 percent) but accepts that under normal conditions, that target cannot be met all of the time. The standards give the expression of that target, and the AQL allows for reality.

The next column is reserved for incentives, if any. Tying incentives directly to the desired outcomes expresses exactly what is important to the company. We discuss incentives in more detail in chapter 9, but suffice to say that the selection and application of incentives is one of the most important details in establishing a Vested Outsourcing program. As Peter Drucker is often quoted, "What gets measured gets managed."

And when the measure determines the financial gain or loss of the person doing the work, that person will do whatever is necessary to achieve that measure. Unfortunately, as we have discussed earlier, improperly designed measures can also create perverse incentives. Keeping the measures in balance is hard work, but it is critical to the effort.

The final section is for recording inspection criteria. It is essential to understand the source for the data, who is responsible for collecting it, and how often. In addition, the specific formula for the calculation of the measure will eliminate later problems and questions. We have seen many cases where transition teams developed an elegant measure, only to learn that the data was not available or required manual extraction and calculation at a prohibitive cost. Because many of these measures will be collected and calculated by the service provider—and new systems often will be configured as part of the transition—this implementation and/or integration of technology represents an excellent opportunity to put in place a data collection method that captures exactly what the team wants. Make these choices early in the process.

ESTABLISH THE STATEMENT OF OBJECTIVES

When the team understands the business model and the workload distribution, it can create the Statement of Objectives (SOO). A SOO is very different from a Statement of Work (SOW).

A SOW defines the tasks to be accomplished and does not allow for much in the way of service provider innovation. The SOW details the work the contractor will perform and, in many cases, how it will be performed. SOWs are *not* performance based and are to be avoided.

A Statement of Objectives allows for the greatest input from the supplier, by asking for innovative solutions to achieve the desired outcomes. The SOO does not list any tasks. The supplier also can propose the plan by which the outcomes will be measured. Essentially, the SOO is designed to provide the contractor with maximum flexibility. Note, however, that some constraints may be in place, and should be identified in the SOO as appropriate.

For example, constraints may include technology acquisitions that might need to conform to company information technology architecture and accessibility standards. Other possible constraints may include security, privacy, and/or safety. The SOO should also identify existing company policies, directives, and standards that are constraining

Figure 8.8   Requirements Roadmap

| Desired Outcome | Performance | | | | Inspection | | | |
	Objective	Standard	Tolerance/ AQL	Monthly Incentive	Who	Data Source	Calculation	How Often Collected
Foodservice that eliminates subsidized costs to the company, and increases utilization by employees	Eliminate company subsidy immedi-ately	For standard cafeteria (6AM–2PM)	None	None	Corp Acct'g dept	Invoicing system	No subsidy to be charged on monthly invoice	Monthly
		For catering services	None	None	Corp Acct'g dept	Invoicing system	No subsidy to be charged on monthly invoice	Monthly
	Increase utilization rate of employees who eat in the cafeteria at lunchtime	Target levels: Yr 1–57% Yr 2–62% Yr 3–64% Yr 4–66%	Target level must be achieved to earn incentive. Targets do not change even if exceeded in prior year	$5,000/ month for each 1% above specified target level	Corp HR & Supplier	Cash Register transactions for time period 11AM–2PM	Average weekly transactions (by supplier) divided by average weekly full-time employees (by HR)	Collected weekly, posted monthly, evaluated quarterly

Pricing to employees should remain at or below established benchmark	Benchmarks (value to be established) • Hot entrée • Sandwich • Salad bar • Pizza	Benchmark value can be adjusted semiannually for changes to consumer price index	None	Corp program manager	Posted menu in cafeteria	Compare current pricing against benchmarks and record variance	Collected monthly, reviewed in QBR (quarterly business review)

factors. However, team members should work with stakeholders to confirm whether these constraints truly are essential or if they have outlived their usefulness. As a final check, examine every requirement carefully and delete any that are not essential, and search for process descriptions, or "how" statements, and eliminate them.

Based on the SOO, the supplier then develops the Performance Work Statement (PWS). This process of moving from SOO to PWS allows the supplier maximum flexibility to solve the problem, including the labor mix. The company can define the results to be achieved and then solicit a wide variety of technical solutions from suppliers. The requirements (desired outcomes and objectives) must be measurable, and performance incentives must be tied to the achievement of performance results (impact of outputs). These results may include cost, timeliness, quality, and impact of outputs associated with the supplier's technical solution. Establishing measurable outcomes without specifying the specific tasks establishes maximum flexibility with the supplier on what work is to be done and provides room for innovation. Using measurable performance standards and financial incentives in a competitive environment encourages suppliers to develop and institute innovative and cost-effective ways to perform the work. One last thought: Do not try to write the perfect SOO or the perfect PWS; it does not exist. Do not sacrifice "good" while waiting for "best."

This phase also concludes with a stakeholder review. As stated before, we firmly believe in a gated process, and your stakeholders are the gatekeepers. To conclude this phase, you need to present your key work products to them and gain their consensus and approvals. Exactly what you must present to whom varies from company to company. The next list should be considered as advisory; add to or subtract from it as appropriate for your situation.

CHECKLIST OF KEY DELIVERABLES— ALIGN INTERESTS

- Business model
- Risk analysis
- Best value assessment
- Requirements Roadmap
- Statement of Objectives/Performance Work Statement

As part of this review, it is also important to identify organizational and systemic resistance to your strategy, if any. Is it individual or departmental? Where in the organization does it originate? Do you have the management support necessary to overcome it? After you have identified and analyzed this resistance, you can determine an action plan for overcoming it. Sometimes it is a matter of misunderstanding, and you should update the communication plan with the appropriate messages to sell strategy. Other times resistance may arise from individuals who fear the loss of their jobs, which of course requires other approaches.

It is also important to establish review cycles with your stakeholders to ensure that the strategy is realized.

CHAPTER 9

ESTABLISH
THE CONTRACT

We discussed the Five Rules of Vested Outsourcing in chapter 4. The fourth rule is a properly structured pricing model that provides incentives for the best cost and service trade-offs. One of the difficulties about choosing the right pricing model is that often there is confusion in the team and especially among the contracting members about the different models used to construct a Vested Outsourcing agreement. This confusion is due to the lack of consistency in how terms are applied to specific contract elements. This chapter helps to clear the fog around pricing models by providing a basic vocabulary and set of definitions that companies can use to determine which pricing model and incentive types are best for them. In addition, it provides a framework for helping organizations understand the key attributes of pricing models and determine which model to apply to which type of contract.

SELECT THE PRICING MODEL

It is important to keep in mind two principles when selecting a pricing model.

1. The pricing model must balance risk and reward for both organizations. The agreement should be structured to

ensure that the outsource provider assumes risk only for decisions that are truly under its control.

2. The agreement should put pressure on service providers to provide solutions, not just activities. A properly constructed Vested Outsourcing agreement encourages the service provider to solve the customer's problem. The better the service provider is at solving the company's problem, the more incentives, or profits, the service provider can make. This fact encourages outsource providers to develop and institute innovative and cost-effective methods of performing work to drive down total cost while maintaining or improving service.

As mentioned in Rule #4, it is also important that Vested Outsourcing teams structure their agreements around reducing the total cost of the process being outsourced, not just the costs of the transactions performed by the outsource provider. Outsource relationships have interwoven dependencies that require the service provider to work (and push) the company outsourcing to change internal processes if they are inhibiting the success. The outsource provider is a profit maximizer. This is reasonable, since few businesses are designed to be otherwise. Therefore, explore what your company can do to encourage outsource provider performance to its own benefit and reward that performance with additional profits.

Companies often struggle to select the proper pricing model that will best support the business and still provide the appropriate embedded incentives to the service provider. The pricing model should be based on the appropriate type of contract (fixed price or cost reimbursement) and the incentives used to reward the outsource provider. In addition, the length of the contract and the prospects for stable demand and funding play an important role in the model, because the outsource provider will use all four factors to calculate the price for its services.

THE BASICS: PICK YOUR TYPE OF CONTRACT FIRST

As mentioned, most companies rely on one of two contract types when building a pricing model for their outsource business arrangements: fixed price and cost reimbursement. In both cases, a company is expected to pay the outsource provider for its costs and a profit to perform its services.

In a nutshell, both pricing models have drawbacks. A fixed-price agreement may influence the outsource provider to cut corners, delivering services at minimally acceptable levels. A cost-reimbursement agreement may encourage the outsource provider to overspend, providing more services than really are needed in an attempt to maximum profits. In both approaches, potential perverse incentives may result in excess resource commitment to contract management; these perverse incentives must be avoided. A high level comparison of contract types is shown in Figure 9.2.

Cost-Reimbursement Contracts

Under a cost-reimbursement contract, a company pays its outsource provider the actual costs to perform a service. By definition, a cost-reimbursement contract is a variable price contract, with fees dependent on the amount of service provided over a specified time period. This type of contract is appropriate when it is too difficult to estimate a fixed price with sufficient accuracy and when the outsource provider will not agree to sign up for the risks associated with unknowns. Cost-reimbursement contracts often are used for the development of a new product or service, where the work cannot be clearly specified, or when outside forces (such as weather) will dictate the frequency of provided service (e.g. snow removal).

In addition to paying for actual costs incurred by the outsource provider, the company pays the outsource provider a profit. The profit is paid in one of three ways:

1. A fixed profit fee (often referred to as a management fee)
2. A variable profit, often a fixed percentage markup that is directly linked to the costs (e.g., cost plus 10 percent)
3. A variable profit tied to prearranged targets where the outsource provider is paid incentive fees for achieving desired cost or performance targets

Cost-reimbursement contracts often are referred to as cost-plus contracts, because the company pays for the cost *plus* the profit to the outsource provider. Some cost-reimbursement contracts estimate the total cost for budgeting purposes and to help the company set aside funds for the outsource provider.

One of the primary disadvantages of a cost-reimbursement contract is that the outsource provider has no real incentive to control its costs, especially if the fee is variable based on the actual cost of service. Figure 9.1 depicts a cost-reimbursement contract with a fixed percentage fee tied to costs.

If the fee is a percentage of the costs, then as costs increase, the fee increases. The problem is that if the outsource provider manages to reduce costs, it is effectively penalized by reduced revenue and profits. The result is a win-lose proposition for the outsource provider. Outsource providers are not inherently motivated to bring cost-reduction solutions to their clients.

To address this issue, some companies are coupling various cost-based incentives into their pricing models. In these cases, outsource providers are rewarded with a gainshare for decreasing costs. The company outsourcing and the outsource provider share these savings. As discussed earlier, Vested Outsourcing is more than gainsharing, but gainsharing does play a role in the process. These incentives are discussed in more detail later in this chapter.

Fixed-Price Contracts

In a fixed-price contract, the outsource provider's price is agreed on in advance and is not subject to any adjustments. As such, the price the

Figure 9.1   Cost-Reimbursement Plus Fixed Fee

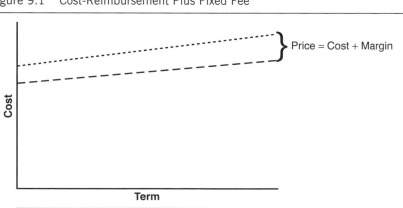

Figure 9.2   Comparison of Contract Types

	Fixed Price	**Cost Reimbursement**
Base Cost	The actual hours and/ or cost of the service are NOT disclosed to the customer by the outsource provider.	The actual hours and cost of the service are disclosed to the customer by the outsource provider and are billed without markup. In some cases, when a third-party provider is involved, the customer may pay that provider directly.
Profit	A management fee/ profit that is added to the cost of the service. This is built into the price the customer pays (with the actual amount usually not disclosed).	A management fee/profit is added to the base cost of the service. This can be a fixed fee, a variable fee (such as a % markup based on costs), or a variable fee based on achieving incentives. It is possible to have a cost reimbursement contract with a zero profit margin where profit is based solely on the outsource provider's ability to perform against desired incentive targets.
Total Cost of Process	The price is agreed on in advance and includes the outsource provider's costs and profit. Typically the outsource provider does not reveal the actual profit margin.	Price is unknown and varies based on the actual costs.

customer pays is fixed and includes the outsource provider's costs and profit. A fixed-price contract eliminates budgeting variation for the company that is outsourcing, either because the amount of service is fixed or because the outsource provider absorbs the peaks and valleys. This type of contract places the maximum amount of risk and full responsibility for costs on the outsource provider. Its ability to manage costs directly impacts its ability to make a profit. The better the outsource provider controls costs, the more profit it can make. Thus, a fixed-price contract provides an inherent incentive for outsource providers to control costs and to put in place process efficiencies that drive costs down.

Fixed-price contracts also are the easiest type of contracts to administer because there is no need for the outsourcing company to keep track of actual costs to determine payment.

The real advantage to a fixed-price contract for a company looking to outsource is predictability of meeting budgets. Remember, all of the risk falls on the outsource provider. One significant disadvantage for the company outsourcing is if the actual cost of providing the services turns out to be less than expected. In this case, the outsource provider "wins" and realizes increased profit margins without having passed over some of the savings to the company outsourcing, and the customer "loses" because it was not able to realize any of the outsource provider's cost savings during the contract. By contrast, if the actual cost of providing the services is higher than anticipated, the outsource provider "loses" and the customer "wins."

This second scenario seldom plays out that way because the outsource provider typically seeks to renegotiate the pricing if it realizes that costs are higher than expected. If renegotiating does not work, the outsource provider has two choices: subsidize the customer's operations or cut costs by reducing service levels in ways not easily detected by the customer. Even if the cost of providing the services is not higher than expected, an outsource provider focused only on the short term may reduce service levels to increase the profitability of the account.[1]

One of the positive elements of a firm fixed-price contract is the *inherent* incentive for the outsource provider to improve the process and costs of providing the services because if its costs are less than the firm fixed price, it will realize a higher profit margin.

We often are asked, "Which pricing model is better?" There is no single right answer. Thought leaders argue the merits of each. In our work, we have seen companies succeed using each solution, so our position is to say rather emphatically, "It depends." The parties must work together to determine which type of contract will best get to the Pony and not lead to the outsourcing ailments.

ROLE OF RISK IN PRICING

Risk is one of the more important criteria in selecting the appropriate pricing model and plays an important role in deciding what contracts are best for your business. Figure 9.3 illustrates how risk transfers from the customer to the outsource provider.

Figure 9.3   Risk Comparison

Source: Adapted from NASA's "Award Fee Contracting Guide," www.hq.nasa.gov/office/procurement/regs/afguidee.html (June 2001).

Under a firm fixed-price contract (depicted on the right in Figure 9.3), the outsource provider is burdened with the maximum amount of risk. It has full responsibility for meeting the contract requirements at the agreed-on price. Under a cost-reimbursement-plus-fixed-fee contract, the company bears most of the risk. The outsource provider has minimal responsibility for the costs, although its fee (or profit) is fixed. In between are contracts in which the outsource provider's profit can be influenced by tailoring various incentive tools to its ability to meet cost and performance (e.g., service-level) targets.

Using incentives can help share risks between a company and the outsource provider and can encourage behavior designed to meet desired outcomes. Researchers from the Wharton School conducted research on performance requirement allocation and risk sharing. The major conclusions were:[2]

- Risk-averse companies are more likely to choose contracts that combine fixed payment, a cost-sharing incentive, and performance incentives than risk-neutral companies, which may prefer performance-based approaches.
- When the company is more risk averse than the outsource provider, the performance incentive increases while the cost-sharing incentive decreases with time. Conversely, if the company is less risk averse than the outsource provider, the performance incentive decreases while the cost-sharing incentive increases with time.
- The allocation of performance requirements and contractual terms changes during the product life cycle. In short,

contracts are likely to evolve, and the mix of contracts will change during the life of the program or the product.

Regardless of the pricing model selected, there is one rule of thumb: The pricing model should not provide the service provider with a given profit margin. Instead, the chosen pricing model should be tied directly to achieving desired top-level performance and cost outcomes.

WHEN TO USE WHICH CONTRACT TYPE

We would be remiss if we did not say that the type of pricing model should be strongly influenced by the nature of the work to be performed. Although there is no standard answer on when to apply which pricing model, you can follow some general guidelines. Figure 9.4 shows several of the different criteria that influence which pricing model a company chooses.

In addition to the criteria shown in Figure 9.4, the type of contract selected should also be based to some extent on the program's maturity level. For example, a well-established outsourced program with a solid baseline and good data might be ideal for a firm fixed-price contract; in the early stages of the Vested Outsourcing efforts, a new program that is just starting and does not have accurate performance or cost data is probably most suited for a cost-plus contract. Later contracts can adjust for the changes in maturity levels.

You can see why we do not say one method is best in all situations. The different criteria in each relationship will lend themselves to one model or another.

FINALIZE THE INCENTIVES

Because both contract types have drawbacks and can produce inherent perverse incentives, a Vested Outsourcing pricing model should intentionally incorporate contractual incentives that are mutually beneficial to both the company outsourcing and the service provider. The challenge in a Vested Outsourcing contract is to find the right incentive to

Figure 9.4   Pricing Model Selection Guidance

Criteria	Favors Firm Fixed Price When...	Favors Cost Reimbursement When...
Level of understanding of the work to be performed	Work is clearly defined	Flexibility to adjust the work tasks is required
Flexibility to adjust work tasks	Regulations or policies will not allow flexibility in tasks	Opportunity to adjust the tasks to gain efficiencies
Ability to influence supplier behavior	Low level of need to influence supplier behavior	High level of need to influence supplier behavior
Level of inefficiency in the operations being outsourced	Current processes are well defined and efficient	High degree of inefficiency in current processes
Budget predictability	Need for predictable budget	Ability to tolerate budget fluctuations to achieve performance goals
Level of understanding of price/high level of competition	Strong competition/high certainty of price	Weak competition/low certainty of price
Need for visibility of cost data	Visibility to cost data is not required	Visibility to cost data is required
Level of confidence in cost data	High level of confidence in cost data and cost history	Low level of confidence in available data and/or cost history
Administrative burden	Low tolerance for administrative burden	Ability to handle administrative burden
Tolerance for risk	High outsource provider risk tolerance Low company risk tolerance	High company risk tolerance Low outsource provider risk tolerance

motivate service providers to make decisions that ultimately will meet the company's desired outcomes.

The concept of including performance incentives in a contract is not new. In 1909, the Wright brothers signed a contract which included these terms:[3]

> Target price: $25,000
>
> Minimum speed requirement: 36 mph
>
> Target speed: 40 mph
>
> Incentive: For every mph over the 40 mph target, the Army would pay an additional $2,500; for every mph under the target, the Army would deduct $2,500, down to the 36 mph minimum, below which point the contract was void.

The results: The final delivered speed was 42 mph, and the Wright brothers earned an additional $5,000.

Although coupling incentives to a contract is not new, getting it right is easier said than done. As we discussed in our description of the ailments that a Vested Outsourcing agreement is subject to, the wrong incentive structure can result in perverse incentives with undesirable outcomes. One of the most common questions companies ask when they are embarking on a Vested Outsourcing contract is: How exactly do I price the contract so that I am really fostering a win-win relationship with my outsource provider? Developing the pricing model that aligns the organizations involved is probably one of the hardest parts of a Vested Outsourcing initiative. Organizations implementing Vested Outsourcing often revert to their win-lose thinking when it comes time to develop the contract—probably because this is when the contracting professionals and lawyers enter the scene. For this reason, we recommend that whoever is negotiating for your company (including the lawyers) is part of the team early on. We also highly encourage the parties involved in Vested Outsourcing to develop the pricing model jointly.

With this in mind, Jeanette Nyden, attorney & president of J. Nyden & Co., Inc. and the author of *Negotiation Rules!* noted: "Developing a pricing model that works for both companies, while fostering a win-win relationship, requires company negotiators to consistently and persistently discuss areas of mutual interest beyond the immediate cost of the service. Focusing on mutual gains prevents much of the posturing that leads to win/lose negotiations."

Game theory proves the value of joint development. O. E. Williamson, a noted expert in the field of transaction cost economics, in contrasting "strategizing" (bargaining, bidding, etc.) with "economizing" (positive sum, efficiency enhancing, etc.), concluded that "economy is the best strategy. That is not to say that strategizing efforts to deter or defeat rivals with clever ploys and positioning are unimportant. In the long run, however, the best strategy is to organize and operate efficiently."[4] In Vested Outsourcing, the customer and the supplier need to choose the rules of the game (the contract), think through the different scenarios and potential outcomes, and examine the outcomes to determine if both sides are pleased with the results. In an effort to improve the process continuously, everyone should ask: what could we do to achieve a better outcome?

Regardless of the type of contract, Vested Outsourcing should use incentives to balance the downsides of each type of pricing model, as discussed in Figure 9.5.

Incentives allow a company to influence directly an outsource provider's profitability by using a predetermined formula that pays additional profit (or reduces profit) based on the outsource provider's meeting agreed-on performance targets. Profit increases are provided

Figure 9.5   Pros and Cons of Incentives

Pros of Incentives	Cons of Incentives
Incentives: – Promote excellent results and outcomes – Promote internal quality control and remedies – Encourage expertise, teamwork, partnering – Encourage supplier satisfaction/ pride in workmanship Monetary incentives: – Promote upper management participation – Promote cost savings Nonmonetary incentives: – Promote workforce satisfaction and stability	Providers with market power can resist them They are difficult to use in contracts, even for experts Exogenous factors can influence performance More work to administer Conflicting incentives can drive suboptimization Wrong incentives drive wrong behaviors

for achievements that surpass the incentive targets; deductions may be made when targets are not met. Incentives typically are used to:

- Encourage an outsource provider to obtain specific objectives that are predetermined in the contract.
- Discourage outsource provider inefficiency and waste.
- Motivate outsource provider efforts that might not otherwise be emphasized.

Different types of incentives are depicted in Figure 9.6, you can and should add incentives to a standard contract to help drive performance and cost improvements.

Incentives were first used in conjunction with cost-plus–type contracts. However, now they are starting to be applied to fixed-price contracts as well. Regardless of its type, every contract should clearly outline the incentive amounts and the incentive determination formula/methodology. The goal of incentives is to link an outsource provider's profitability directly to the achievement of stated desired outcomes.

We are often asked if it is appropriate to use multiple incentive types for a single contract. The answer is not only it is possible, but in our opinion it is desirable. A properly structured multiple-incentive arrangement should motivate the outsource provider to strive for outstanding results and process innovation to drive costs down. Incentives should be balanced to ensure that perverse incentives are not created, and compel the outsource provider to make trade-off decisions among the incentive areas that are consistent with the desired outcomes. A good contract will use a balanced set of incentives that fosters an environment where the outsource provider does not strive to maximize achievement of one particular objective to the detriment of overall performance.

The number of evaluation criteria and the requirements they represent differ widely among contracts. The criteria and rating plan should motivate the service provider to improve performance in the areas rated but not at the expense of at least minimum acceptable performance in all areas.

It is important to create incentives that are not too cumbersome to track and monitor. Administrative costs should not under any circumstances exceed the expected benefits. If something is hard to measure, you may be suffering from ailment 9, measurement minutiae. In all cases, establish procedures to assess achievement of incentive targets.

Figure 9.6   Incentive Types

Incentive Type	Description
Cost Incentive	A cost incentive takes the form of a profit adjustment and is intended to motivate the outsource provider to manage costs effectively. Cost incentive clauses in contracts should include a target cost, a target profit or fee, and a profit adjustment formula. Typically when an outsource provider meets the stated target cost objectives, it will receive the stated profit target objectives. Actual costs that exceed the target typically result in a downward adjustment to the outsource provider's profit. Actual costs that fall below the target typically result in an upward adjustment of the profit. Cost incentives have either variable or firm targets.
Performance Incentive	Performance incentives typically are tied to the outsource provider achieving a specific desired performance characteristic. The desired performance typically is stated in terms of a quantitative service targets (e.g., % on-time completion) and/or qualitative targets (e.g., customer satisfaction). A performance incentive should be designed to relate the outsource provider's profit to achievement of specific targets. The incentive fee may be fixed or variable but always corresponds to specific, agreed target ranges of service. Fees typically are paid quarterly.
Nonmonetary Incentives	Incentives such as public recognition, case studies, willingness to provide references, and other goodwill gestures are often powerful intangible incentives.
Award Fee	An award fee is an incentive fee paid at the conclusion of a fixed-duration contract for achieving a desired goal. Award fee incentives typically are used when the outsource provider's performance cannot be measured objectively, because the nature of the work makes it difficult to devise predetermined objective incentive targets applicable to cost or performance. Usually this type of contract specifies a given service that is paid regardless of the final outcome, with an award fee added if the service concludes with a desired result. The incentive fee may be variable but usually is fixed.
Award Term	The best contract incentive is always more business, and a service provider always should strive to increase market share. An award term is an incentive that extends the term of the contract without rebidding the work. If the performance meets the agreed targets, the contract is extended, usually for one year. In some cases, this extension occurs annually, with or without an agreed final end date.

Contracts should also provide for evaluation at stated intervals (usually monthly) so that the outsource provider is periodically informed of the quality of its performance and the areas in which improvement is expected. Partial payment fees should generally correspond to the evaluation periods. This review process helps create an environment that induces the service provider to improve poor performance or to continue with good performance. The number of evaluation criteria used in determining whether incentives can be paid, and the requirements they represent, will differ widely among contracts. The criteria and rating plan should motivate the service provider to improve performance in the areas rated but not at the expense of at least minimum acceptable performance in all areas.

Performance and target incentives are integral to Vested Outsourcing. In themselves, they do not create a contract that is performance based but they always should be incorporated to ensure that the outsource provider is working toward the proper goals.

CONTRACT LENGTH

We have talked about contract type and incentives—the third essential element of the contract structure is the contract length. Longer-term contracts encourage service providers to invest for the long haul in business process improvements and/or efficiencies that will yield year-over-year savings, a crucial component of a successful Vested Outsourcing agreement. In many cases, investments in process improvements, such as new equipment or information technology infrastructure, can run into the millions of dollars. Service providers need the ability to forecast their future revenue stream (at least the minimum levels) in order to determine whether the return on investment will be reasonable. The length of the contract should be commensurate with the payback period for a service provider's investment.

Long-term contracts may be needed to get the partners to the Pony. Often, achieving step-level improvements in process efficiencies takes a significant investment on the part of the service provider. Without the assurance of a longer-term contract, often they are unwilling to invest in these process efficiencies.

In addition, longer-term contracts have an intangible benefit to the company outsourcing. If the company spends the proper time selecting the right service provider and structuring the pricing model, it will need to write fewer contracts. The annualized costs associated with writing and developing one 10-year contract are substantially cheaper than creating two 5-year contracts and much less than creating five 2-year contracts. Given the scarce resources within most organizations and continued downsizing of most corporate functions, it is even more critical that contracts are for longer periods of time.

STABLE DEMAND AND FUNDING

The last element of the contract structure should be a mutual understanding of how stable the demand and the funding will be over the life of the contract. Because all organizations face volatility in business and are challenged with budget constraints, it is realistic that firm volume commitments cannot always be promised to the service provider. We recommend that Vested Outsourcing contracts have minimum volume thresholds that allow the service provider to cover fixed costs or at least create a pricing model that allows for fixed costs to be covered regardless of transactions or volumes. Service providers will shy away from making investments in the business if they feel that their potential revenue streams might be reduced during the life of the contract.

The price the service provider eventually charges will be in direct correlation to its level of confidence in its ability to earn future revenue. If the company and the service provider do not have a common understanding of how stable future funding is for the work, the service provider likely will add a risk premium to the price. It is in the best interest of the company outsourcing to provide solid estimates (and if possible minimum levels) of commitment.

Let us use an example of Alpha Company, which has experienced a tough first quarter due to lower-than-expected holiday sales. Operational budgets were cut by 50 percent, and a freeze was placed on all logistics support for a four-week period in order to help the company manage costs.

But the pain doesn't stop there. The contract service provider for Alpha Company, Beta, had a significant amount of fixed costs in its long-term agreement. Under a transactional-based pricing model, Beta did not receive any revenue for the four-week period and had to absorb the fixed cost expenses. If the contract would have been short-term, Beta would likely cut staff, or even canceled the contract, leaving Alpha

Company without the necessary support to ramp up when business improved. But under a long-term agreement, Beta can justify short-term expenses against a long-term potential gain, especially when it has confidence in Alpha's three year plan.

PUTTING IT ALL TOGETHER: SOME GENERAL TIPS

As we have said, it is important to recognize that the outsource provider is and should be a profit maximizer. Consider what you can do to motivate outsource provider behavior that leads to benefits for you, and reward that behavior appropriately.

Focus on the Big Picture

At some point during the life of the contract, assuming the team has found the Pony, someone in finance or senior management is likely to observe that the outsourced provider's gross profit margin is exceeding industry norms. Often this person overlooks the investment that the provider had to make to achieve these margins. Most likely, this person will make this observation in emphatic terms and request that the contract be renegotiated. It is important to remember the big picture and the fundamentals that drive Vested Outsourcing. As we have stated, it is not only OK, it is *essential* that the service provider get larger gross profit margins. It has earned the profit by investing and helping the company get its part of the Pony.

Utilize Present Value Leverage to Drive at the Base Profit

Most Vested Outsourcing thought leaders advocate that any fixed fee that is included in an agreement (a fixed price or the fixed profit in a cost-plus agreement) be somewhat below market norms, for two reasons. First, this stipulation guarantees the company outsourcing some of the Pony up front. The company gets an immediate cost reduction by moving to the Vested Outsourcing agreement because the service provider puts skin in the game. The outsource provider is more or less betting that it can use its brainpower to deliver the Pony. Second, it keeps the outsource provider hungry for additional profit and will provide a natural incentive for it to drive toward process and technology improvements, which is where the real Pony is found.

As we mentioned, we recommend longer-term contracts, a mini-mum of three years and up to five or even ten years. Contracts of this length allow the outsource provider to trade off immediate cost reduc-tions in the base fee for the opportunity to secure additional profits in future periods. We have seen 10-, 15-, and even 20-year contracts; the outsource provider's large investments warranted a long payback period in which to recoup its investment. Simply put, a long-term contract has real value to the service provider, and you should not just hand those benefits over. The service provider must apply its brainpower to tap into the profit potentials of these additional years of the contract.

Do Not Cap the Incentive

Another tendency in contract negotiation is to rebaseline the savings targets every year. In essence, the company insists that the outsource provider finds new cost savings annually in order to earn that year's incentives. Such behavior is not acceptable in a Vested Outsourcing agreement. As discussed in chapter 3, this drives ailment 6, sandbagging: withholding gains that could have been achieved earlier. Sandbagging benefits no one and often deprives the outsourcing company of substan-tial gains. Cost savings and service improvements should be measured, judged, and incented over their full duration, usually the full term of the contract.

Pricing Models Should Mature

In many situations, it makes sense for the Vested Outsourcing rela-tionship to mature over time. This is especially true when there is limited baseline information for the service provider to identify the Pony. As the service provider gains more experience, the company can evolve to a contract type that transfers more risk (and reward) to the provider.

One company that we studied had an evolution strategy to migrate more and more risk to the service provider over the life of the contract. In Phase 1, the contract was quasi–performance based with somewhat tighter-than-usual specifications and a gainshare linked to shared cost savings. The detailed specifications gave the company a comfort level of control but limited the service provider's flexibility and ability to inno-vate for cost improvements. In addition, the shared cost savings became a point of contention. If the company's personnel suggested a way to save costs to the service provider, and the service provider did the evaluation and implementation, the service provider would rightly claim the savings. The company had a different viewpoint, as it had identified the potential savings; situations like this led to many contentious discussions.

In Phase 2, the Vested Outsourcing agreement moved the contractual arrangement to a results-based focus, with the emphasis on achievement of goals. The incentives were changed to put at risk the service provider's management fees (essentially, its profit). However, the potential for greater service provider profits was also built in. If the service provider's performance met expectations, the profit margin was similar to that of the first contract. But if the service provider was able to exceed goals, including cost reductions, it could earn a higher profit. Again, the goal was cost reduction, and the burden was put on the outsource provider to reduce those costs. The tight specifications in the first contract limited creativity and the ability to bring best practices to the table. The second contract encouraged consideration of a wider range of possible alternatives.

In Phase 3, the Vested Outsourcing contract was global in nature. It included all services in different parts of the world under a single umbrella and leveraged the global spend of key service providers. The incentive structure closely followed the model established in the second contract, which has proven to be quite successful for this company.

OFF-RAMPS AND REOPENER CLAUSES

A central principle of Vested Outsourcing is mutual trust between parties. It is a mutual, beneficial, symbiotic relationship. Successful Vested Outsourcing relationships are most certainly not the traditional adversarial relationships inherent in legacy contract approaches. Thus, at the time of contract negotiation, often potential conditions are not fully addressed. Rather than spending significant effort in negotiating detailed clauses to cover every potential eventuality, a Vested Outsourcing relationship relies on a shared commitment to the desired outcomes outlined in the Performance Work Statement and a willingness to work through challenges when they become real. "Unfortunately, many relationships begin to deteriorate at the first sign of trouble," Nyden explained. "In order to prevent this from happening, each company should engage in genuine fact finding rather than nitpicking. If tensions are running high, consider bringing in someone with professional facilitation skills to conduct an in-person meeting."

Not all contracts—or relationships—will stand the test of time. For this reason, a contract should always include off-ramps and reopener clauses. The contract should allow for modifications or cancellation should circumstances change. If the company outsourcing or service provider is not living up to expectations, the other party should be able to exit the contract without protracted negotiation or litigation.

In a positive and productive Vested Outsourcing relationship, the parties should never need to terminate for cause or convenience. In the interest of completeness, however, we describe these traditional termination approaches and their application.

Termination for Cause

In a termination for cause, one party has failed to live up to its contractual commitments, and both parties may experience economic consequences. A company that is outsourcing may choose to terminate a commercial contract for cause for two reasons:

1. The service provider did not comply with contract terms and conditions.
2. The service provider failed to provide the outsourcing company with adequate assurances for future capabilities or performance.

Prior to terminating a contract for cause, the outsourcing company should create a "cure notice" with the service provider, specifying the exact details of the concern and the time allotted for correction; the service provider then has to come up with a plan to fix the problem within the time allowed.

Should the service provider fail to remedy the situation, the outsourcing company may choose to proceed with the contract termination, in which case it will issue a "show cause notice". This notice will warn the service provider of the impending contract termination and request that the service provider provide reason and/or rationale for the contract not to be terminated.

Although termination for cause can be considered an off-ramp, it should be avoided. A termination for cause can follow a service provider around, much like the proverbial Scarlet Letter. It also can reflect badly on the outsourcing company if the service provider makes a convincing case of innocence to the informed public.

Termination for Convenience

While not recommended, the outsourcing company traditionally has a right to terminate a contract if it is determined to be in the company's best interest. However, the company should have a very good reason to terminate a contract. When doing so, the outsourcing company must provide to the service provider a written statement of the reason for the contract termination as well as a settlement agreement and a final accounting for all matters that relate to the termination. Some reasons for convenience terminations might include:

- Insufficient funds available
- Elimination of the requirements
- Reduction in quantity needed
- A major change to the requirements that is beyond the service provider's ability to perform
- Acquisition of the outsourcing company or merger with another company

Although it is the right of the outsourcing company to use a termination for convenience, the service provider is protected since the outsourcing company must compensate it for any work performed, including a reasonable profit.

Additional compensation factors may also include the return of assets, compensation for assets acquired, and compensation for service contracts for equipment. In addition, certain key service provider personnel may have formed close relationships with the company's customers and/or have significant knowledge that the company must reacquire or transfer to a new provider. However, the most important thing to remember is that neither company is operating in a vacuum but both are part of a team. Open, two-way communication between company and provider is crucial in maintaining a good working relationship: In your Vested Outsourcing contract, be sure to include clearly written, very specific exit criteria as negotiated options.

VESTED OUTSOURCING IMPLEMENTATION

As important as a sound Vested Outsourcing strategy is, it is equally important to implement a good method to monitor and manage the program once the planning and negotiating is completed. Programs—like babies—don't grow on their own. At this point in the game, the few critical metrics should have been established and agreed on. Managing performance is simply a matter of having an effective way of monitoring metrics attainment and implementing any revisions necessary to ensure success. This step is a service provider's lifeblood. Without sound measurement tools and accurate reporting of both primary and supporting metrics, the provider risks letting the hard-earned profits slip away.

Rule #5 (discussed in chapter 4) states that the governance structure of a successful Vested Outsourcing agreement is established to provide insight, not merely oversight. To provide this insight to the management team, we recommend the implementation of a comprehensive and detailed quality assurance plan, based on the Requirements Roadmap. At a bare minimum, the quality assurance plan should include:

- The metrics used to measure the service provider's performance and support outcomes, such as system availability, reliability, and process performance
- The period of performance upon which incentive evaluations will be based
- The parties responsible for collecting, compiling, calculating, and assessing the metrics
- The specific data sources from which the metrics will be derived
- How the metric values will be scored, weighted (if applicable), and prioritized to calculate the amount of the contractual incentive
- How disputes over assessment data will be resolved

Because the only constant is change, it is important for service providers to work closely with the company's program manager. Service providers must be proactive in an ever-changing environment and constantly review and adjust the metrics to ensure a win-win program.

Some of the most successful programs have used an incremental progression approach to adopting a Vested Outsourcing business model. Having a strategy to migrate to Vested Outsourcing rather than simply flipping a switch from a traditional model to the new business model allows both parties to ease into the new method of outsourcing. In addition, often baseline data is not available for the program being outsourced. Creating a bridge contract allows service providers to assume activities or responsibility for the component, subsystem, or platform while not requiring them to take on full risk. Under this scenario, it is common for bridge contracts to continue to be cost plus in nature, but service providers are asked to actively track metrics and create a solid program baseline. As a program matures, it should evolve to a business model that shifts the risks and rewards of managing the sustained process to the service providers.

CHECKLIST OF KEY DELIVERABLES— ESTABLISH THE CONTRACT

- Pricing model
- Incentives
- Contract
- Quality assurance plan
- Transition plan

CHAPTER 10

MANAGE PERFORMANCE

The contract is in place. You are ready to hand over everything to the new outsourcing partner and walk away, because you are done, right? Wrong! Remember what we said about giving birth? Now is when you understand why we have been insisting that the people who are going to manage this partnership long term be part of the team from the beginning.

A study conducted by the Outsourcing Center identified the two largest factors in outsourcing failures:

1. The buyer's unclear expectations up front as to its objectives: 23 percent.
2. The parties' interests are aligned up front but become misaligned as the buyer's business environment or needs change: 15 percent.[1]

In another research report, Technology Partners International, Inc. surveyed 40 companies across multiple industries that had restructured or renegotiated outsourcing contracts. The goal of the research was to understand why the restructuring was undertaken and to capture key lessons from the companies' experiences. Figure 10.1 shows companies' agreement with these statements. Clearly, signing the contract is just the beginning.

So far we have focused on defining expectations, but as the ballplayer Yogi Berra once said, "It ain't over till it's over!" Throughout the Vested Outsourcing process, the people who will manage this

Figure 10.1   Reasons for Restructure

Statement	Agreement
Placing more emphasis on setting up the contract than managing it	61%
Service provider(s) failed to deliver on promises	53%
Unrealistic expectations on the part of the organization	52%
Inexperience at managing outsourcing contracts	49%
Unrealistic expectations on the part of the service provider	37%
Source: Technology Partners International, Inc., "Restructuring Outsourcing Agreements" (The Woodlands, TX, 2007).	

partnership should be part of the team in order to acquire the background and knowledge necessary to be successful. Failure to involve the process owners early in the process offers a fertile environment for unclear expectations to continue unabated.

TRANSITION

Somewhere between signing the contract and the everyday management of its functions, a transition occurs. It may be a transition from a company-operated function to a new supplier, from an old suppler to a new supplier, or maybe just a new way of doing things between the same parties that have been doing the work all along.

Outsourcing suppliers are very knowledgeable regarding transitions, but it is important to emphasize several points:

- Plan the transition.
- Leverage the relationship.
- Celebrate the successes, if possible.

Enter into the new relationship with a positive attitude and a clear emphasis on the good things in store for both companies if you work together in partnership. As we have mentioned, this relationship should be viewed more like bringing on a new employee than like buying a service. But we do want to underscore a few key points in the transition phase:

- Keep the team together.
- Communicate and train.
- Implement supplier relationship management.
- Conduct quarterly business reviews.
- Implement continuous improvement.
- Evaluate the effectiveness of your strategy.

Keep the Team Together

The team involved in the performance management of the Vested Outsourcing process should not be a new one; it should be a sourcing team that is transitioning to a performance team. The team we have described throughout this process was an integrated solutions team comprised of all participants in the outsourcing. It included representatives from the technical, supply, and procurement communities and the customers they serve. The team also included representatives from the suppliers that will provide the products and/or services, but probably not as full team members with access to all communications and information. The suppliers are now an integral part of what is to occur and should be integrated as full team members.

For the process to be successful, at least a core of the integrated solutions team must remain. This group has the most knowledge of why things are structured as they are and what has to happen next. Their roles will change and adjust to new post-contract award roles, and their responsibilities will need to be remapped as required. Learning the business is very different from keeping it.

Some outsourcing companies will feel that since the function has been outsourced, it is no longer necessary to keep any technically skilled managers on staff. This is a very dangerous path to follow, as it results in abdication as opposed to supplier management. As mentioned earlier, the supplier may ask some of the key players to join their management team. Other managers may leave for new opportunities. But certain important outsourcing company managers must remain in place to manage the partnership. There is a fine line between delegating responsibility to the supplier while remaining accountable for the results and managing the supplier so tightly that you might as well not have outsourced the process at all. Both of these methods are preferable to tossing the process over the wall and walking away. It still takes high-powered talent in the company to gain the most benefit from Vested Outsourcing.

A manager responsible for a facilities management contract now entering its third phase under a Vested Outsourcing agreement made several observations about the "stay-behind" team—the group members who remained with the company to manage the outsource provider. Paraphrasing, the manager pointed out:

- Being on the team was initially difficult for most of the people. They essentially were being told they were not good enough at their jobs.
- It was difficult at first not to micromanage, to tell the supplier how to do its job, or to nitpick small problems. The group members had to shift their thinking to managing the supplier instead of managing the supplier's people.
- Overall, these difficulties were outweighed by the expertise and longtime experience that the group members brought to the process, but they did have to modify their behaviors to be successful.

Communicate and Train

The program manager must communicate implementation and transition strategies and any new business rules to users and stakeholders. You should not underestimate the need to conduct required training and education—remember, you have been part of this process redesign all along, and fully understand it, but the customers of the process were probably not as involved, and do not understand many of the changes in "how we do things here." You will need to educate not only customers but also any new contract administration personnel. You will also need to appoint and conduct formal training for the quality assurance personnel who will be responsible for implementing the performance plan.

An implementation kickoff meeting is a good place to start. This meeting gives the team a chance to celebrate, provides an opportunity to introduce the supplier to additional users and stakeholders, and sets the tone for the transition. Make the meeting upbeat and positive, stressing the desired outcomes and their impact on the business and relationship with your new business partner.

Remember, this is a partnership, a new phase in outsourcing. It is a team working together and learning from each other. Start positive and stay positive. The first step for the company is to implement a program in supplier relationship management (SRM) if one is not already in place.

Implement Supplier Relationship Management

SRM is a comprehensive approach to managing an enterprise's interactions with the organizations that supply the goods and services it uses. The goal of SRM is to streamline and make more effective the processes between an enterprise and its suppliers. This is not formalizing a structure for assigning blame if/when things go wrong but the establishment of processes for communication, reporting, and improvement.

SRM practices create a common frame of reference to enable effective communication between an enterprise and suppliers that may use quite different business practices and terminology. As a result, SRM increases the efficiency of processes associated with acquiring goods and services, managing inventory, and processing materials. Some key elements of this transition are shown in Figure 10.2.

Figure 10.2   The Transitions of SRM

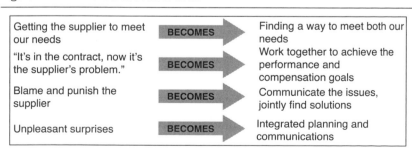

Getting the supplier to meet our needs	BECOMES	Finding a way to meet both our needs
"It's in the contract, now it's the supplier's problem."	BECOMES	Work together to achieve the performance and compensation goals
Blame and punish the supplier	BECOMES	Communicate the issues, jointly find solutions
Unpleasant surprises	BECOMES	Integrated planning and communications

Source: Adapted from a presentation by Expense Management Solutions, "Complex Outsourced Services: A Strategic Framework," Institute for Supply Management presentation, May 2007.

Communication is key to the success of SRM. Many companies insist on using traditional hierarchical communication where everything flows through the outsourcing company's program manager and the supplier's account manager, as shown in the FROM diagram in Figure 10.3, sometimes referred to as the Bow-Tie model.

We strongly encourage a change to direct functional communication through the appropriate contacts in the respective organizations, as shown in the TO diagram in Figure 10.3, with managers of individual components responsible for keeping the company's program manager and the supplier's account manager fully informed. It is essential that the managers hear about problems from their teams first, though, rather from their superiors who received the information from their peers in the other company. If they do not, the relationship is doomed.

We know from experience that this communication model improves the flow of information and helps to empower the teams. This flow of information should be specified in the partnering agreement/guiding principles established between the outsourcing company and the service provider. Resist the temptation—and/or pressure from upper management—to revert to the Bow-Tie method at the first breakdown.

As with any team, regularly scheduled conference calls and team meetings are the grease for the wheels. Governance involves free-flowing communication between operational groups, their managers, and executives of both companies. The most successful teams talk daily, weekly, monthly, and quarterly, as suggested in Figure 10.4.

Quarterly Business Reviews

The last row on Figure 10.4 refers to the quarterly business reviews (QBRs) that should be conducted among the company, the supplier, and the key stakeholders. These meetings are the means for reviewing progress against the desired outcomes, and to appraise and approve earn-outs on incentives. Large acquisition programs should use data-driven analysis as the basis for contractor communications and reviews. The goal is to actively manage and drive performance. A sample agenda for this meeting is presented next.

Figure 10.3   Communication Model

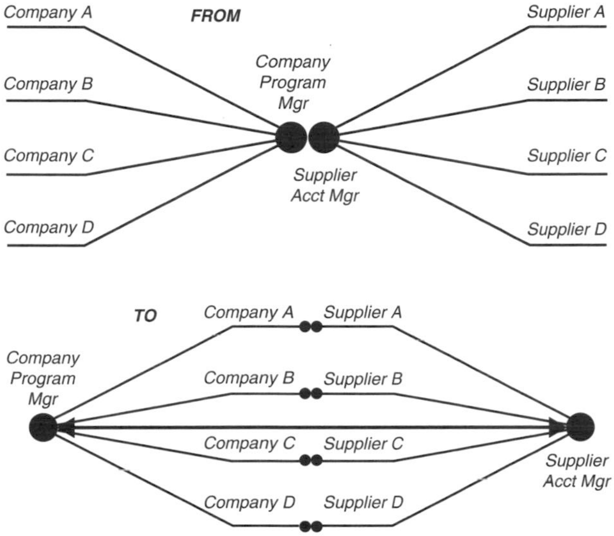

Figure 10.4   Meeting Structure

Frequency	Purpose	Attendees
Daily	Address issues as they arise. • Short stand-up meeting first thing in the morning and/or last thing before going home. • Phone calls as needed.	Functional team leads
Weekly	Progress check/weekly metrics. • What the metrics are showing. • Issues, if any. • Discuss upcoming events and/ or issues that are coming up at other companies.	Program manager, account manager, functional team leads
Monthly	Review monthly metrics, performance, and issues.	Departmental managers, program manager, account manager, functional team leads
Quarterly	Full Quarterly Business Review (QBR). Formal agenda including performance against desired outcomes, incentives, and trends (see sample agenda).	Corporate managers, departmental managers, program manager, account manager, functional team leads

Data-Driven Quarterly Business Review Agenda

   Performance to requirements
     Review of requirements attained
     Analysis of any requirements not met
       Trend of requirements
       Understanding of trends; Pareto chart or similar graph of
        why not met
       Root cause identification/solution
       Action plan/steps taken to improve trend, eliminate cause
        for not meeting requirement
     Analysis of attainment of benefits projected in the
      business case
   Business analysis
     Identification of any new business trends affecting the partnership
     Review of any business case requiring investment to improve
      service or decrease costs
     Action plan/timeline for implementation
     Feedback from customers, supplier, and/or other stakeholders
   Requirements update
     Any new requirements added over the last quarter
     Any future plans for requirements changes
   Appendix
     Organizational information
     Metrics definitions
     Detailed key performance indicator (KPI) reporting by program

Implement Continuous Improvement

Continuous improvement is the heart and soul of most successful performance improvement programs. This raises two questions:

1. Why would we say any more about it?
2. Why isn't everyone already doing it?

In the interest of the second point, we will say a little, but in the interest of the first point, we will keep it short. Continuous improvement is best facilitated by a never-ending series of changes. There will always be the need and the opportunity to supplement enterprise strategies and initiatives with such changes. The process should be simple and constructive, not complex and potentially destructive. Working together as a team to implement continuous improvement projects also increases the bond between the team members and promotes good communication. The incentives created should recognize that these continuous improvement efforts will be taking place and should reward the attainment of the improvements in the incentive structure.

Begin by formulating a plan for managing continuous improvement. Assign team members roles and responsibilities for managing the process. Everyone and anyone can offer ideas for improvement. Define the process for submitting and evaluating ideas, and communicate it to everyone who touches the process: customer, user or service provider. Under the guidance of the program manager, the team must then evaluate and prioritize the ideas according to the potential for achieving or exceeding the desired outcomes and act on the high-potential ones. And be sure to collect feedback from the stakeholders and review it to evaluate your continuous improvement strategy.

Evaluate the Effectiveness of Your Strategy

You began this journey with a defined set of desired outcomes, based on your business strategy. Are you still on course? Has your business strategy changed? In addition to continuous improvement, you need to analyze continually your strategy and your performance using performance-based objectives and metrics.

Begin by asking yourself some simple questions: Why did we do this? Are we achieving the goal? Are we achieving the right outcomes? Remember our discussion example on strategy in cafeterias? There we asked such questions as:

- Are health costs going down?
- Are people staying at work to have lunch, or are they leaving the building?
- Are operating costs going down?
- How do we know?

We have spent the last five chapters talking about getting this Vested Outsourcing agreement in place, and managing it on an on-going basis. One last thought—what happens at the end of the contract? On one hand, if the partnership is structured properly, is achieving the desired outcomes and continually improving performance and profitability for both companies, the contract will be renewed time and again. On the other hand, few relationships continue this way indefinitely, so you must prepare for harsh reality.

One of the potential dangers of outsourcing is becoming so intertwined and dependent on the service provider that the potential benefits of changing to a new provider cannot match the pain of extraction. This situation occurs most often when management of suppliers shifts to abdication to suppliers. By maintaining proper management control and a balanced relationship between company and supplier, two very good things happen:

1. There is less likelihood of the partnership degrading.
2. You retain the ability to dissolve the partnership as required by new circumstances.

It is in the best interests of both the company and the service provider to work toward this ongoing balanced partnership.

CONCLUSION

The significant problems we face cannot be solved at the same level of thinking we were at when we created them.
— Albert Einstein

Our goal in writing this book is to encourage outsourcing professionals—including those in companies that outsource and those at service providers—to take Einstein's advice and think beyond conventional transaction-based outsourcing business models in search of a better way to outsource. We hope that after reading this book you begin to face your outsourcing opportunities with a new level of thinking and embrace Vested Outsourcing as a means of developing better relationships with your suppliers and customers.

We would also like you to keep in mind that a true collaborative outsource environment can be created only where there is respect for people. Vested Outsourcing brings collaboration to a new level but requires a significant change in mind-set. It requires not only a meeting of the minds but also a clear understanding of what is to be expected.

For those of you choosing to take the challenge, Tim McBride, Microsoft's chief procurement officer, offers this advice:

As a leader in innovation, Microsoft is always quick to experiment with new approaches. Our first approach with Vested Outsourcing concepts was in the area of facilities management with Grubb & Ellis, and we have been quite pleased with the results. In fact, Grubb & Ellis has won both the supplier of the year and the environmental supplier of the year under this approach. We are definitely seeing the benefits of a collaborative, measurement-focused relationship that drives both Microsoft and Grubb & Ellis toward the achievement of common goals and objectives. For Microsoft, the next step will be to learn from our lessons and apply Vested Outsourcing philosophies across other areas that we are outsourcing.

The one thing that we have definitely learned is that saying win-win is much easier than acting win-win when it comes to dealing with suppliers. Most procurement professionals are hard wired to win, which means if Microsoft wins, the supplier loses. We have learned that applying a Vested Outsourcing philosophy requires a cultural change in how we will need to work with our suppliers. For Microsoft, this means exploring Vested Outsourcing one program and one supplier at a time—working to build trust with our supply base and business units that outsource to understand that there really is a better way.[1]

We hope that our collective wisdom as practitioners and academics, coupled with our research, has provided insight for helping take your outsourcing relationships to the next level. We believe those who challenge themselves to follow the Vested Outsourcing rules will create innovative solutions that resolve the conflicting goals so often found in conventionally outsourced business models. The rules of Vested Outsourcing should be the foundation for your outsourcing arrangement.

As you invest in your Vested Outsourcing relationships, ask yourself these questions to determine if you are really thinking about a balanced win-win contract:

- Will the company outsourcing reduce its overall cost of the entire solution?
- Will the service levels improve or stay the same (unless there is a strategic direction to reduce service levels to reduce costs)?
- Will the service provider improve its margin if it is able to achieve service-level and cost objectives?

Ultimately, you should be willing to change places with the person sitting on the other side of your outsourcing deal and feel good about it.

We also encourage you visit the Vested Outsourcing web site, www.VestedOutsourcing.com, to download the implementation tools and resources we have referred to throughout the book. Of course, we also invite you to Knoxville, Tennessee, to join us for one of our upcoming classes.

ACKNOWLEDGMENTS

I n writing *Vested Outsourcing*, we stood on the shoulders of sovi many talented people that it is hard to know where to begin to express our gratitude. Except, perhaps, at the place where this book began: with the research.

Alex Miller of the University of Tennessee: You involved us in the research at the beginning, listened to the vision, and encouraged us to keep pushing the envelope.

Blaise Durante: You pushed the Air Force to improve and opened doors to allow us to assist the organization in the pursuit of excellence.

The staff of the U.S. Air Force, including General Wendy Masiello, Colonel Mark Hobson, Colonel Dave Searle, Marie McManus, Edie Ryan, Lieutenant Colonel Chris Moore, and Sandy Schwartzwalder: You spent many hours critiquing and contributing to our efforts to develop performance-based service acquisition courseware for your teams.

Dan Stewart of the University of Tennessee: You drove the research initiatives, coordinated the resources, provided the executive-level insights, and generally marshaled the tasks that kept everything moving forward.

Steve Brady, Steve Rutner, Steve Geary, and Mike Winchell: Thanks for being part of the University of Tennessee research team in various capacities. Your contributions to the team were invaluable.

John Riblett, Bric Wheeler, and Karen Hanlon from the University of Tennessee: You were always there, helping us manage the projects, procure the materials, and generally assist the research efforts as we developed the concepts that are core to Vested Outsourcing.

Lyle Eesley from the Defense Acquisition University: Who else could have provided the breadth of vision and experiences with the various services to help keep us aligned in our mission?

Thanks to all of the progressive organizations that provided us with case studies, best practices, and a vision for excellence: They must remain unnamed due to many of their corporate rules and competitive advantages, but we could not have perceived and defined the potential gains without them. You know who you are, and you have our deepest gratitude.

Elizabeth Kanna: You offered the vision for what could be and the tools and guidance necessary to make that vision a reality.

Laurie Harting: You were quick to understand the power of Vested Outsourcing and provided valuable strategic direction on this book. With Palgrave Macmillan, we truly have a vested relationship!

Bill DiBenedetto and the Palgrave editor Erin Ivy: Thanks for reining in our jargon, smoothing out our disjointed writing styles, and making us sound like one pleasant voice for change.

Steve Symmes, Steve Murray, and Joe Tillman: Thanks for your hours of diligent research and documentation of concepts that saved us days and days in our journey.

Thanks also to the following thought leaders who reviewed our work along the way and provided valuable feedback, support, and endorsement that Vested Outsourcing truly is a game-changing business model that will define how companies outsourcing in the future:

AFMS, Logistics Management Group, David Humes
Boeing, Beth Schindelar and Megan Weinstock
Booz Allen Hamilton, Joe Talik
CEVA Logistics, Kim Wertheimer and Lester Grubbs
Council of Supply Chain Management Professionals, George
  Gekowitz, former CEO
CTSI, Cliff Lynch
DC Velocity, Mark Soloman
Dell, Anton van Steenwijk and Michael Connor
Fujitsu Consulting, Mike Riegler
Georgia-Pacific, Stephen Carney
Intel, Todd Shire
IWLA, Joel Anderson
Logistics Quarterly, Fred Moody
Microsoft, Rachel Henney and Tim McBride
Penton Media, Perry Trunick
Plan4Demand, Andrew McCall
Reed Publishing, Frank Quinn
State of Georgia, Kevin Gekowitz
Supply Chain Visions, Bill Keough

The University of Tennessee, David Ecklund
Warehousing Forum, Ken Ackerman

A special thanks to Adrian Gonzalez of ARC Advisory Group and Frank Casale of the Outsourcing Institute for taking up the cause and pushing it forward. You have been cheerleaders of the concepts of Vested Outsourcing from Day 1. You are both true visionaries in the field.

To Mike Watts, Rhonda Watts, Laurie Hanley, and Karen Wiley: You keep Kate organized, on time, and everything running in perfect order for her. You are a savior for Kate, and for that we are all indebted.

And last, but certainly not least, to our families, for all your support and patience during this fabulous experience:

Greg and Austin Picinich
Kris, Megan, Amy, Jason, Holly, and Max Ledyard
Susan, Katie, Sarah, and Ben Manrodt

NOTES

INTRODUCTION

1. Thomas M. Koulopoulos and Tom Roloff, *Smartsourcing: Driving Innovation and Growth through Outsourcing* (Avon, MA: Platinum Press/Adams Media, 2006).

1 THE WHOLE NINE YARDS

*Kate Vitasek the main author.

1. Stream International was a large, diverse service provider that provided technical support, call center services, software manufacturing, and other operational services primarily to the high-tech industry. In 1997, the manufacturing and operational arm of Stream International spun off into a division known as Modus Media International. CMGI acquired Modus Media International in 2004 and merged it with its SalesLink division to form ModusLink. In 2008, the parent company was renamed from CMGI to ModusLink Global Solutions.
2. Craig R. Carter, P. Liane Easton, David B. Vellenga, and Benjamin J. Allen, "Affiliation of Authors in Transportation and Logistics Academic Journals," *Transportation Journal* 48.1 (Winter 2009): 42–52.
3. Kate Vitasek, Stephan Brady, Mike Ledyard, Karl Manrodt, and Lyle Eesley, "Performance-Based Acquisition Research Findings," University of Tennessee, 2009.
4. Memorandum from the Under Secretary of Defense, Acquisitions, Technology and Logistics, "2005 Secretary of Defense Performance-Based Logistics Awards," October 21, 2005.
5. Adrian Gonzalez, "The Green (and Social Media) Side of Con-Way's TrueLTL Pricing," ARC Advisory Group, Logistics Viewpoints, July 22, 2009.
6. K. C. Jones, "Sprint Nextel Sues IBM over Outsourcing Deal Gone Bad," *Information Week,* May 25, 2006; www.informationweek.com/news/global-cio/showArticle.jhtml?articleID=188500738.
7. Jeff Boudreau and Brad Sampson, "When 'Insourcing' Is the Right Choice," *CSCMP Supply Chain Quarterly* 1.2 (2007): 62–67.
8. Frank Casale, "Outsourcing 2.0: The New Outsourcing and What It Means to You," *Outsourcing Institute* (2000): 1.
9. Adapted from Ben Zimmer, "Where Did We Get 'The Whole Nine Yards'?" Word Routes. Visual Thesaurus. March 25, 2009. Retrieved April 2009 from

http://www.visualthesaurus.com/cm/wordroutes/1783/. Benjamin Zimmer, "Great Moments in Antedating" (HTML). June 21, 2007. Language Log. University of Pennsylvania. Retrieved April from 2009http://itre.cis.upenn. edu/~myl/languagelog/archives/004623.html. Gary Martin, "Thc Whole Nine Yards—Meaning and Origin," *Phase Finder* (2006). Retrieved April 2009.

2   AN OUTSOURCING PRIMER

1. Adam Smith, "An Inquiry in to the Nature of the Wealth of Nations." 1776. Retrieved May 2009 from http://www.bartleby.com/10/101.html.
2. C. Lonsdale and A. Cox, "The Historical Development of Outsourcing: Latest Fad?" *Industrial Management & Data Systems* 100.9 (2000): 444.
3. T. Peters and R. Waterman, *In Search of Excellence* (New York: Harper & Row, 1982).
4. C. K. Prahalad and Gary Hamel, "The Core Competence of the Corporation," *Harvard Business Review* 68.3 (1990): 79–91.
5. Thomas Friedman, *The World Is Flat: A Brief History of the Twenty-first Century* (New York: Farrar, Straus, and Giroux, 2007).
6. Michael Corbett, *The Outsourcing Revolution* (Chicago: Dearborn Trade Publishing, 2004), p. XV.
7. Ibid.
8. Ruben Melendez, "Outsourcing ROI: Key Elements and Benchmarks for Obtaining Maximum Results," *Industry Week,* June 11, 2008.
9. International Association of Outsourcing Professionals, IAOP Web site. Retrieved March 2009 from www.outsourcingprofessional.org/content/ 23/196/1683.
10. Editorial Staff, "Emerging Markets Driving Continued Growth in Global Business Process Outsourcing Market," Supply and Demand Chain Executive Online. June 2008. Retrieved June 2009 from http://www.sdcexec.com/ online/article.jsp?siteSection=13&id=10482&pageNum=1R.
11. Yuskavage, Strassner, and Medeiros, "Domestic Outsourcing and Imported Inputs."
12. J. Harvey and P. Brudenall, "Risky Business, High Payoffs," *Forbes,* May 29, 2008.
13. Melendez, "Outsourcing ROI."
14. Deloitte Consulting Outsourcing Advisory Services, "Why Settle for Less?"
15. PricewaterhouseCoopers, "Outsourcing Comes of Age: The Rise of Collaborative Partnering." 2007. Retrieved March 2009 from http://www. pwc.com/en_GX/gx/consulting-services/pdfs/outsourcingcomesofage. pdf.
16. Deloitte Consulting Outsourcing Advisory Services, "Why Settle for Less?" 2008. Retrieved March 2009 from http://www.deloitte.com/dtt/cda/doc/ content/us_consulting_oaspovwhysettle_141207%281%29.pdf.

17. P. Roehrig, "Bet on Governance to Manage Outsourcing Risk," *Business Trends Quarterly* (2006). Retrieved March 2009 from http://www.btquarterly.com/?mc=bet-governance&page=ss-viewresearch.
18. Melendez, "Outsourcing ROI."
19. Deloitte Consulting Outsourcing Advisory Services, "Why Settle for Less?"
20. "The Second Decade of Offshore Outsourcing: Where We're Headed," *Information Week,* November 5, 2007.
21. 'Winner's Curse' Affects 20% of Outsourcing Deals," *Computer Business Review,* September 26, 2006.
22. IAOP Web site.
23. Kathleen Goolsby and F. Keaton Whitlow, "What Causes Outsourcing Failures?" *Outsourcing Journal* (August 2004).
24. Deloitte Consulting Outsourcing Advisory Services. "Why Settle for Less?" 2008. Retrieved March 2009 from http://www.deloitte.com/dtt/cda/doc/content/us_consulting_oaspovwhysettle_141207%281%29.pdf.
25. Michael G. Vann, "Of Rats, Rice, and Race: The Great Hanoi Rat Massacre, an Episode in French Colonial History," in *French Colonial History,* vol. 4 (East Lansing, MI: Michigan State University Press, 2003), 191–203.

3   TEN AILMENTS OF TRADITIONAL OUTSOURCE RELATIONSHIPS

1. Vince Elliot, "Task-Frequency Specs: Time for a Change?" *CM Cleaning Management Magazine* (October 1991).
2. Bill Bryson, *A Short History of Nearly Everything* (New York: Broadway Books, 2003).
3. Kate Evans-Correia, "Gartner: Outsourcing Deals Based on Price Alone Are Likely Doomed," CIO.com, March 15, 2006.
4. Michael Redding, "Managing the Risks of Facilities Management Outsourcing," *Real Estate Weekly,* June 7, 2006.
5. Tim McGrath, "The Legendary Sergy Bubka." *Inside Athletics,* April 8, 2009, pp. 22–24. Retrieved from http://issuu.com/insideathletics/docs/ia08final?mode=embed&layout=http%3A%2F%2Fskin.issuu.com%2Fv%2Flight%2Flayout.xml.
6. Aberdeen Group, "The Invoice Reconciliation and Payment Benchmark Report: Elevating the Value of the Order-to-Pay Process," Aberdeen Group. June 2004. Retrieved May 2009 from http://www.aberdeen.com/summary/report/benchmark/invoicereconciliation.asp.
7. "Best Practices in E-sourcing—Optimizing and Sustaining Supply Savings," Aberdeen Group, September 2004. Retrieved from http://www.aberdeen.com/summary/report/other/bp-esourcing.asp.
8. "Local Government Finance Formula Grant Distribution—A Consultation Paper," chapter 5 in *UK Department for Communities and Local Government* (2002).

9. James C. Robinson, "Reinvention of Health Insurance in the Consumer Era," *Journal of the American Medical Association,* April 21, 2004.

4   CHANGING THE GAME:
THE RISE OF VESTED OUTSOURCING

1. Best Manufacturing Practices Center of Excellence, "Best Practice: Preferred Supplier Program," Best Manufacturing Practices, September 2006. Retrieved March 2009 www.bmpcoe.org/bestpractices/internal/nges/nges_36.html.
2. Brad Stone, "Best Buy and TiVo Are Forming an Alliance," *New York Times Online.* July 2009. Retrieved July 9, 2009 from http://www.nytimes. com/2009/07/09/technology/companies/09tivo.html.
3. Note: Although we use the term *both parties* frequently throughout this book, not all Vested Outsourcing agreements involve only two parties. There could be three or more parties in one agreement. For the sake of uniformity, *both* is commonly used.
4. M. M. Sathyanarayan, *Offshore Development: Proven Strategies and Tactics for Success* (Cupertino, CA: Globaldev Publishing, 2003).
5. Chris Owens and Michele Flynn, "Locking in the Benefits of Outsourcing: Innovation, Cost Reduction, and Continuous Improvement at Microsoft," *Leader* (September 2005): 2–5.
6. Ibid., 5.
7. U.S. Department of Defense Performance-Based Logistics Award for Excellence, nominations submitted July 2007.
8. Department of the Navy, Commander, Naval Supply Systems Command, nominations for the Secretary of Defense Performance-Based Logistics Award, July 6, 2005. http://thecenter.utk.edu/cms/Sub-System+Award+ Nominations/612.html.
9. Quotes from Douglas Lee, "Digging in the Dirt for FOI Gold." September 1998. Retreived from http://www.freedomforum.org/templates/document. asp?documentID=7515.
10. J. Collins and J. Porras, "Building Your Company's Vision," *Harvard Business Review* 74.5 (1996): 65–77.

5   THE GAME-CHANGING
ECONOMICS OF VESTED OUTSOURCING

1. The Effect of Marital Status on Stage, Treatment, and Survival of Cancer Patients, James S. Goodwin, MD; William C. Hunt, MA; Charles R. Key, MD, PhD; Jonathan M. Samet, MD (JAMA 1987;258:3125–3130, from http:// www.psychpage.com/family/library/brwaitgalligher.html).
2. Linda J. Waite and Maggie Gallagher, *The Case for Marriage: Why Married People Are Happier, Healthier, and Better off Financially,* PyschPage.com. Retrieved May 2009 from www.psychpage.com/family/library/brwaitgalligher.html.

3. Nobel Prize Press Release, Retrieved March 2009 from http://search.nobelprize.org/search/nobel/?q–nash&i=cn&x=10&y=10, (*Nobelprize.org*).

4. B. Cole, "Bill Gates Could Gain a Lot from a Little Game Theory," *EE Times,* June 19, 2000.

5. R. Axelrod and R. Dawkins, *The Evolution of Cooperation*, rev. ed. (New York: Basic Books, 2006).

6. Cole, "Bill Gates Could Gain a Lot from a Little Game Theory."

7. N. Angier, "Why We're So Nice: We're Wired to Cooperate," *New York Times,* July 23, 2002.

8. R. Wessel, "More M.B.A. Programs Embrace Game Theory," *Wall Street Journal,* March 31, 2006.

9. Koehn, Daryl. "Business and Game-Playing: The False Analogy," *Journal of Business Ethics* 16.12/13 (September 1997): 1447–1452.

10. Mikhael Shor, "Nash Equilibrium," Dictionary of Game Theory Terms, Game Theory.net. Retrieved March 2009 from http://www.gametheory.net/dictionary/NashEquilibrium.html.

11. A. Brandenburger and B. Nalebuff, *Co-opetition* (New York: Doubleday, 1998).

12. "Innovation Is Essential for Your Economic Growth," Clerical Business Solutions. Retrieved April 18, 2009 from http://clericalsolutionsinc.net/default.aspx.

13. Cynthia Barton Rabe, *The Innovation Killer* (New York: Amacon, 2006), p. 12.

14. A.G. Lafley and Ram Charan, *The Game Changer* (New York: Crown Business, 2008), p. 216.

15. Jena McGregor, with Michael Arndt and Robert Berner in Chicago, Ian Rowley and Kenji Hall in To, "The World's Most Innovative Companies." *Business Week* 39.81 (April 2006): 63–74.

16. Mark Blaxill and Ralph Eckardt, *The Invisible Edge: Taking Your Strategy to the Next Level Using Intellectual Property* (New York: Penguin Group, 2009), 104.

17. Alireza Naghavi and Gianmarco I.P. Ottaviano, "Outsourcing, Complementary Innovations and Growth," Center for Economic Policy Research, Working Paper 19 (May 2008).

18. Alan MacCormack, Theodore Forbath, Peter Brooks, and Patrick Kalaher, "Innovation through Global Collaboration: A New Source of Competitive Advantage," Harvard Business School, Working Paper 07–079 (August 2007). p. 3.

19. Lafley and Charan, *Game Changer.*

20. Marisa Brown, "Best Practices in Innovation: Lessons Learned from the Leading Edge," APQC. Retrieved April 20, 2009 from www.apqc.org/portal/apqc/ksn/APQC_PharmaMfgMag=134620.

21. Larry Huston and Nabil Sakkab, "Connect and Develop: Inside Proctor & Gamble's New Model for Innovation," *Harvard Business Review* 84.3 (March 2006): 58–66.

22. Lafley and Charan, *Game Changer.*

23. Frank Pager, trans., *Venetian Patents (1450–1550) by Guilio Mandich, Journal of Patent Office Society* 30 (1948): 166–224.
24. Blaxill and Eckardt, *Invisible Edge,* 42.
25. Quote by Abraham Lincoln, *Complete Works of Abraham Lincoln* 5 (1894): 113.
26. Paul Romer, "Endogenous Technological Change," *Journal of Political Economy* 98 (1990): S71–102.
27. Robert Solow, "Technical Change and the Aggregate Production Function," *Review of Economics and Statistics* 39 (1957): 312–320.
28. Jacob Schmookler, "The Changing Efficiency of the American Economy," *Review of Economics and Statistics* 34.3 (August 1952): 214–231.
29. Blaxill and Eckardt, *Invisible Edge,* 44.
30. Intel., 2005. Video Transcript "Excerpts from a Conversation with Gordon Moore: Moore's Law." *Intel Corporation.* Retrieved from ftp://download.intel. com/museum/Moores_Law/Video-Transcripts/Excepts_A_Conversation_ with_Gordon_Moore.pdf.
31. Blaxill and Eckardt, *Invisible Edge,* 64.
32. Ibid., 160.
33. Jeffrey Dyer and Kentaro Nobeoka, "Creating and Managing a High-Performance Knowledge-Sharing Network: The Toyota Case," *Strategic Management Journal* 21 (2000): 345–367.
34. Ibid.
35. Blaxill and Eckardt, *Invisible Edge,* 166.
36. Ibid., 162–164.
37. MacCormack, Forbath, Brooks, and Kalaher, "Innovation through Global Collaboration."

6 LAY THE FOUNDATION

1. Corbett, *The Outsourcing Revolution* (Chicago, IL: Dearborn Trade Publishing, 2004).
2. Edgar H. Schein, *Organizational Culture and Leadership* (San Francisco: Jossey-Bass, 1986).
3. Robert Solow, "Technical Change and the Aggregate Production Function," *Review of Economics and Statistics* 39 (1957): 312–320.
4. "Creating Organizational Transformations: McKinsey Global Survey Results," *McKinsey Quarterly* (August 2008).
5. This definition is from a Balanced Scorecard Institute online glossary. BSI derived it from a Government Accountability definition: "Stakeholder: An individual or group with an interest in the success of an organization in delivering intended results and maintaining the viability of the organization's products and services. Stakeholders influence programs, products, and services. Examples include congressional members and staff of relevant appropriations, authorizing, and oversight committees; representatives of central management and oversight entities such as OMB [Office of Management and Budget] and GAO [Government Accountability Office];

and representatives of key interest groups, including those groups that represent the organization's customers and interested members of the public."
6. BBC News—Asia Pacific, "Square Fruit Stuns Japanese Shoppers," June 15, 2001, http://news.bbc.co.uk/2/hi/asia-pacific/1390088.stm.

7   UNDERSTAND THE BUSINESS

1. "CSCMP Supply Chain and Logistics Terms and Glossary," Council of Supply Chain Management Professional (Chicago, August 2009).
2. Lewis Carroll, *Alice's Adventures in Wonderland* (London: Macmillan, 1865).
3. A.G. Lafley and Ram Charan, *The Game Changer* (New York: Crown Business, 2008), p. 212.

8   ALIGN INTERESTS

1. A.G. Lafley and Ram Charan, *The Game Changer* (New York: Crown Business, 2008), p. 144.

9   ESTABLISH THE CONTRACT

1. "Facility Management Pricing Models," Grubb & Ellis Company white paper (2007).
2. "'Power by the Hour': Can Paying Only for Performance Redefine How Products Are Sold and Serviced?" *Wharton School* (February 2007): 3–4.
3. Defense Acquisition University, Continuous Learning Center, Online Module CLL011, "Performance-Based Logistics" (2005).
4. O. E. Williamson, "Strategizing, Economizing, and Economic Organization," *Strategic Management Journal*, 12, Special Issue: Fundamental Research Issues in Strategy and Economics (Winter 1991): 75–94.

10   MANAGE PERFORMANCE

1. Kathleen Goolsby and F. Keaton Whitlow, "What Causes Outsourcing Failures?" *Outsourcing Journal* (August 2004): 1.
2. A Pareto chart is a graph that shows the most frequently occurring problems or sources of problems in descending order.

CONCLUSION

1. Research interview.

INDEX